THE RETAIL REVOLUTION

THE RETAIL REVOLUTION

*Market Transformation,
Investment, and Labor
in the Modern Department Store*

BARRY BLUESTONE
PATRICIA HANNA
SARAH KUHN
LAURA MOORE

Social Welfare Research Institute
Boston College

 Auburn House Publishing Company
Boston, Massachusetts

Prepared under the auspices of the Joint Center for Urban Studies of MIT and Harvard University, this book is based on a report prepared for the Office of Economic Analysis and Research, Economic Development Administration, U.S. Department of Commerce, under grant number OER-620-G78-14 (99-7-13440). The work was co-sponsored by the Office of Research and Development, Employment and Training Administration, U.S. Department of Labor; and the Center for the Study of Metropolitan Problems, National Institutes of Mental Health, U.S. Department of Health, Education, and Welfare. The statements, findings, conclusions, and recommendations herein do not necessarily reflect the views of any of the sponsoring agencies.

Library of Congress Cataloging in Publication Data

Main entry under title:

The Retail revolution.

Bibliography: p.
Includes index.
1. Department stores. I. Bluestone, Barry.
HF5461.R47   658.8′71   80-26036
ISBN 0-86569-052-9

Printed in the United States of America.

PREFACE

This book on the department store industry is based on a case study completed under a broad program of research on economic development. The program was sponsored by the Economic Development Administration of the U.S. Department of Commerce, the Employment and Training Administration of the U.S. Department of Labor, and the Center for the Study of Metropolitan Problems, a division of the National Institutes of Mental Health of the U.S. Department of Health, Education, and Welfare. The original research was undertaken at the MIT-Harvard Joint Center for Urban Studies in cooperation with MIT's Department of Urban Studies and Planning and its Sloan School of Management, and with the Social Welfare Research Institute at Boston College. The long list of sponsors and the number of universities involved in the project give some idea of the immense magnitude of the research initially undertaken.

The original project was built upon the premise that one can only understand the dynamics of an economy by understanding the nature of its industries. The research staff, under the direction of Professor Bennett Harrison of MIT, opted early for an analytic strategy based on individual industry case studies. The small set of industries chosen for investigation was carefully selected on the basis of each industry's contribution to the region in terms of employment generation and its overall role in economic development. The department store industry was selected for study because of its economic contributions in terms of employment generation, its overall role in economic development, its explosive growth in the post World War II era, and its significance as a major employer of women.

Perhaps because most of us spend some portion of our lives in department stores and therefore have some surface familiarity with the industry, none of us on the research project was at the outset particularly enthusiastic about the prospect of spending a year studying what appeared to be a rather nondescript sector of the economy—

no matter how many jobs it provided. Studying the aircraft industry, computers, or even the world of shoe manufacturing seemed to promise a much more exciting research adventure. To our delight, however, our initial perceptions turned out to be dead wrong. Department stores, as the reader will discover, have a fascinating history in America worthy of a good novel or two, let alone a scholarly treatise. The dynamics of the industry, far from being dull and routine, tell us more about capital investment and the labor process in the United States than do many of the nation's premier manufacturing industries. Indeed, there is as much to learn about industrial behavior by studying retail trade as there is in a study of the automobile or steel industry.

Surprisingly, the transformation of department stores from locally owned and operated "petite bourgeoisie" enterprises to billion-dollar international conglomerates is chock-full of the same kind of intrigue that characterized the development of small 19th-century manufactories into the mammoth multinational industrial conglomerates that dominate today's economic landscape. It is at once a story of rampant competition, the pyramiding and collapse of financial empires, the innovation of space-age technology, and the reorganization of work and the labor process. The difference is that the revolution in retail trade is a matter of current events, not history. It is, accordingly, in some ways more instructive, for it is our own generation's history.

The methodology we use—an industry case study—is unique. Business schools are known for their use of the case method, but their studies are usually of a particular firm or even a division of an enterprise, not an entire industry. Economists, on the other hand, seldom ever look into the "black box" called the firm or the industry. They tend instead to look at abstract markets, not the complex institutions which operate within them.

In our case, we have deliberately focused on the actors in the market system—on the enterprise managers and their market strategies, on the workers who sell and stock merchandise, and on the government which regulates much of the whole business. The story told here is how these actors and institutions have evolved as the result of competitive pressures and political struggle. We have been particularly careful to detail how the competitive battle is actually fought in this industry, and how the outcome of the competition affects the nature of jobs and the labor process, as well as the consumer who is the ultimate target of the entire retail system.

As we completed our reworking of the original manuscript to better reflect the nationwide stature of the department store industry, we became more fully aware of just how crucial industry case studies may become. The issue of "the reindustrialization of America," as *Business Week* recently put it, burst on the economic scene as unemployment continued to grow without much let-up in the rate of inflation.* The domestic automobile crisis and increasing international penetration in this industry and others suddenly began to attract political attention. For the first time in nearly fifty years, there was widespread alarm about the productivity of the U.S. economy and the country's ability to maintain economic growth and prosperity.

The need for a better understanding of just how the economy works, and especially how individual sectors and industries operate, finally became fully recognized. To guide economic policy, at least one member of the U.S. Congressional Joint Economic Committee, Representative Henry S. Reuss, called for "independent teams from government, business, and labor . . . to look into the problems of each of our major sectors . . . with the objective to devise sectoral policies and develop plans covering corporate restructuring, new investment and its location, remedial regulatory legislation, and public financial assistance where required."† While retail trade has not reached the point of crisis as in other sectors, it seems not too early to begin the inquiry suggested by Representative Reuss. It is our hope that this book will be seen as a step in this direction.

BARRY BLUESTONE
BOSTON COLLEGE
SEPTEMBER 1, 1980

---

* "The Reindustrialization of America," Special Issue, *Business Week* (June 30, 1980).
† *Ibid.*, p. 87.

ACKNOWLEDGMENTS

Every step in the development of this book benefited from the nurturance of our colleagues at MIT, Harvard, and Boston College. New England Economy Project staff meetings held at the Joint Center for Urban Studies helped us formulate questions and untangle mysteries as they arose in our research. While all of the staff gave us help at one time or another, special thanks are due Professor Bennett Harrison, the project's Principal Investigator. Ben gave us constant encouragement and, on many occasions, coaxed us to probe deeper into complex issues.

Our promise of strict anonymity to our industry sources prevents us from listing the names of the dozens of company officials, industry experts, and union officials who gave of their time and insight so that we might bolster this research with fresh information and accurately reflect the current status of the industry. Our personal thanks are offered to all of you.

As for our own staff at the Social Welfare Research Institute, we want to express once again our gratitude. Special thanks are due Alan Matthews, Ann Grenell, Tom Barbera, Mark Cullinane, Amy Kruser, Susan Fahlund, and Tim Benell who helped us all along the way. Finally, the four of us wish to express our deepest appreciation to Virginia Richardson who supervised the overall production of the monograph that became the basis of this book.

CONTENTS

List of Figures   xii

List of Tables   xiv

CHAPTER 1
Introduction   1

Description of the Department Store Industry   3
Methodology of the Study   7

CHAPTER 2
A History and Taxonomy of the Department Store Industry   10

Modes of Retail Trade: A Taxonomy   15
   Department Store Chains   15
   Discount Department Store Chains   18
   The National Holding Company   23
   The Independent Department Store   26
   The Specialty Store   27
The Struggle Between Modes of Retail Trade   29

CHAPTER 3
Macroeconomics, Demographics, and the Fate
   of Retail Trade   36

Population   37
Per Capita Income   44
Consumer Credit   46
Technological Change and Other Factors   47
Market Concentration in the Department Store Industry   48

Regional Growth and Decline   50
Trends in Department Store Profits   51
Retail Saturation and Regional Markets   54

CHAPTER 4
Ownership, Capital Investment, and Expansion in the
    Department Store Industry   61

Two Forms of Ownership: Private and Corporate   61
    "Bigness," Economies of Scale, and the New Corporate
    Structure   64
Capital Sources   66
    Geographic Movement of Capital   68
Growth Patterns Within the Department Store Industry: Buy-
    outs and Diversification   70
    Expansion into the Suburban Market   70
    Expansion of the Central City Market   71
Methods of Expansion   72
    Retail Expansion into Nonretail Areas   74
    Expansion of Nonretail Firms into Retail Areas   76
    Expansion into Foreign Markets   76

CHAPTER 5
The Department Store Labor Force: Trends, Turnover,
    and Tenure   80

Part-Time Employment   82
Turnover and Tenure in the Labor Force   84
The Origin of the Workforce   87
The Destination of the Labor Force   89
Long-Run Trends in Labor Mobility   92

CHAPTER 6
Earnings, Productivity, and the New Technology
    of Retail Trade   98

Earnings in the Department Store Sector   99
    Minimum Wage Laws and Labor Costs in the Industry   106
    The Decline in Commission Selling   109
The Role of Unions   110
Training   111

Productivity and Technology 112
   Transportation, Advertising, and Productivity 115
Productivity and Employment 117

CHAPTER 7
The Role of Government 120

Robinson-Patman Price Discrimination Act of 1936 120
Fair Trade Laws: Resale Price Maintenance 124
Recent Legislation 128
Blue Laws 129
The Paradox of Government Policy 131

CHAPTER 8
The Role of Management 133

The Management Factor 134
Why Firms Fail 137
An Industry "Wish List" 139

CHAPTER 9
Summary and Conclusion 143

The "Industrialization" of Department Stores 143
Advertising, Technology, and Government Policy: Returns to
   Bigness 146
Transformation of the Labor Market and the Labor Process 148
The Future of the Department Store Industry 149

Bibliography 152

Index 155

LIST OF FIGURES

2.1 Concentration in the Discount Department Store Industry, 1966 to 1977   21

3.1 Regions and Divisions of the United States   39

3.2 Net Interregional Migration 1965–1970 and 1970–1975   41

3.3 Population Forecasts to Year 2000 by Region   43

3.4 Per Capita Income by Region, 1960–1978   44

3.5 Net Income/Sales Ratio for 32 Largest General Merchandisers, 1963–1977   52

3.6 Net Income/Sales Ratio for 5 Largest General Merchandisers, 1963–1977   53

3.7 Number of Households per Discount Store in the United States and Regions   56

3.8 Number of Households per Discount Store in the New England States   57

3.9 Number of Households per Store by Region, 1967–1978   58

5.1 Employment in the New England Department Store Industry, 1957–1975   82

5.2 Percentage of Department Store Employees Under Age 25   96

6.1 Age Earnings Profiles of White Men, 1957–1975   102

6.2 Age Earnings Profiles of White Women, 1957–1975   104

6.3 1975 Earnings Distribution for Year-Round Workers in the New England Department Store Industry, by Sex   106

6.4 1957 Earnings Distribution for Year-Round Workers in the New England Department Store Industry, by Sex   107

6.5 Real Sales and Employment in the New England
Department Store Industry, 1963–1977 118
7.1 Cost to Buyer Under Indirect and Direct Selling 123

LIST OF TABLES

1.1	U.S. Retail Trade Components, 1967–1978	5
2.1	Sales Volume by Retail Trade Mode, 1960–1977	19
2.2	The Size Distribution of Discount Department Store Chains, 1966–1977	22
2.3	Modes of Production in the Department Store Industry—Operations, Control, and Structure	30
3.1	Population by Region, 1950–1975	38
3.2	Per Capita Income (Current Dollars) by Region, 1963–1977	45
3.3	Percentage Change in Real Department Store Sales (1967 Dollars) by Region, 1963–1977	46
3.4	Consumer Credit: 1950–1977	47
3.5	Concentration in the General Merchandise Industry Sales, 1967, 1977	49
3.6	Growth Index for Leading Retailers (1963 = 1.00), 1963–1977	49
3.7	Growth Among Department Store Modes (1963 = 1.00), 1963–1977	50
3.8	Dun & Bradstreet Random Sample of Department Stores in New England by Mode of Ownership, 1969, 1972, 1974	51
3.9	Average Net Income/Share Equity Ratios for Leading Department Store Firms, 1963–1977	53
3.10	Gross Change in Number of Department Store Establishments in New England, 1969–1976	59
5.1	Turnover in the Department Store Industry, 1950's–1970's	84
5.2	Tenure in the Department Store Industry (Origin = 1968)	85

5.3   Separation and Accession Rates in New England
      Department Stores, 1957–1975   85

5.4   New England Department Store Average Separation
      and Accession Rates, 1957–1975   86

5.5   Origin of Department Store Employees
      (Destination: 1974)   87

5.6   Origin of Department Store Employees by Sex
      (Destination: 1974)   88

5.7   Destination of Department Store Employees, All
      Employees (Origin: 1974)   89

5.8   Destination of Department Store Employees, Age <
      25 (Origin: 1974)   90

5.9   Destination of Department Store Employees, Age
      35–54 (Origin: 1974)   91

5.10 Industry Origin and Destination of All
      Department Store Employees in New England,
      1974   92

5.11 Industry Origins and Destinations of Department
      Store Employees by Sex in New England, 1974   92

5.12 Destination of Department Store Employees, Age
      Cohort 1958 (Origin: 1958/Destination: 1965)   93

5.13 Destination of Department Store Employees, Age
      Cohort 1968 (Origin: 1968/Destination: 1975)   94

6.1   Annual Earnings (Current Dollars) of Primary Job
      Holders in Department Stores   100

6.2   New England Department Store Industry Annual
      Earnings (Current Dollars) for Full-Year White
      Workers for Whom SIC 531 Was Primary
      Employer, by Age and Sex, 1962–1975   100

6.3   Department Store Industry Real Wages
      (1967 = 100) for Full-Year White Workers for
      Whom SIC 531 Was Primary Employer, by
      Age and Sex, 1957–1975   101

6.4   Percentage Real Wage Increases for Full-Year
      Primary Workers by Age, Race, and Sex, 1957–1975   101

6.5   New England Department Store Industry Earnings
      (Current Dollars) Distribution for Full-Year Workers
      by Sex, 1975   105

6.6   Advertising and Personal Commodity Consumption
      Expenditures, 1950–1976   115

6.7   Advertising Expenditures by Medium   116

6.8   Aggregate Sales, Employment, and Payroll in New
           England Department Stores, 1963–1977   117

Chapter 1

INTRODUCTION

At first glance, the department store industry appears to be a sleepy backwater in the sea of corporate America. The folksy, unsophisticated management style of the old-time general store lives on in the imaginations of today's consumers. Despite striking changes in store size, range of merchandise, and selling practices, we easily presume that what goes on in the back room of a modern-day department store is not significantly different from the management styles and goals of a century ago. In fact, however, a dramatic and fundamental transformation has taken place in the department store industry since the turn of the century. The early *petite-bourgeoisie* form of merchandising has given way to corporate forms of retail ownership and management which bear more resemblance to corporate structures such as General Motors and AT&T than they do to the small, independent businesses from which they sprang. It is the purpose of this book to examine the history and nature of this radical transformation, and to explore its consequences for the industry, for labor, for consumers, and for the regional and local economies that provide department stores their markets.

The inclusion of almost all aspects of human life in the market economy is a relatively recent phenomenon. As more and more goods which were formerly produced by individuals and families for their own consumption become instead commodities to be bought and sold in the marketplace, retail trade has expanded and has become increasingly central to the conduct of life itself. In 1979 the department store industry alone had annual gross sales of $89.1 billion.[1] Top management of the largest department store firms receive salaries appropriate to an industry of this size and comparable to those paid to the heads of major nonretail corporations. The department store industry, heir to the general store and specialty store of the 19th century, is now very big business indeed.

1

Many of the changes now taking place in the retail industry are recapitulations of changes which took place in manufacturing industries a generation or more ago. This study examines the most prominent aspects of the process which might be called the "industrialization" of department stores. Ownership patterns have become increasingly concentrated, moving in the direction of retail oligopoly, while at the same time many department store firms have diversified their holdings. A variety of forces, including economies of scale, the advanced technology and mass advertising available to large firms, government regulation, and the financial backing of large corporate parent firms have contributed to uneven development within the industry.

As in the industrial core of the economy—in steel, auto, rubber, and electrical goods long ago—the giants of the department store industry have swallowed up most of the once-prominent smaller independents, or have, through the competitive marketplace, driven them out of business. The use of labor within the department store has also changed, with skill requirements dramatically reduced for most sales jobs. The experience and knowledge of trained salespeople has given way to the almost mechanical skills of the "order taker" and processor of commodities. The check-out clerk has become like the worker on an industrial assembly line. Warehousing, data processing, ordering, and many managerial tasks have been "rationalized" in the large firms, again mirroring earlier developments in manufacturing.

An apparent contradiction in the industry's transformation is that while the structure of the industry became more oligopolistic during the 1960's and 1970's, the department store market grew more competitive, not less. The competition between giant retailers is being fought out through ceaseless efforts to cut costs wherever possible. Competition also produces tremendous pressures on firms to expand geographically in order to capture a larger segment of the overall retail market. But as history shows, the rush to preempt other stores in the acquisition of choice locations can be the key to success or the road to failure for a retail firm. In a highly competitive market, the drive to grow and to cut costs brings about fundamental changes in employment practices, capital structure, investment, and the use of technology. These forces, as well as others discussed in the chapters which follow, have dramatically changed the face of the industry over the last two decades.

An important outcome of the rapid consolidation of department store firms around the country is that the industry is now composed of many national, as opposed to local or even regional, enterprises.

Large department store firms move in a national capital market and make their investment decisions at the national and now even the international level. Within firms, capital tends to move from more highly "saturated" to less costly, less developed regions. This practice, while it allows capital to be invested where it will earn the greatest return, promotes social and economic dislocation not unlike that left in the wake of steel or auto plant shutdowns in recent years. Commitment to a neighborhood or a region, the norm when retailing firms were small family-owned businesses, is rare in large national firms. Instead, individual department store units compete with branches in other regions and indeed with investment opportunities overseas for capital from the parent company. Shrinking returns on investment in older, more saturated areas lead large national corporations to transfer capital to other regions and eventually out of retail into other sectors of the economy.

These changes in the industrial structure of retail trade have had a profound impact on the industry's demand for labor. Management's desire to reduce costs has led to repeated efforts to reduce the firm's dependency on labor. The result is an increasingly polarized wage structure, with a low-skilled, high-turnover workforce at the bottom of the pyramid and a highly trained professional-managerial group at the top. The substitution of advertising and technology for labor, combined with a reduction in the proportion of jobs in the industry which are full-time, has effectively eliminated employment opportunities of career caliber at the low end of the industry hierarchy.

In the pages which follow, these recent trends within the industry are examined in detail. The history of department stores, the changing structure of the industry, the determinants and effects of increasing competition and concentration, the implications of demographic change, the impact on labor, and the roles of government and management are all part of this story. Each of these is an aspect of the retail revolution.

Description of the Department Store Industry

According to the Standard Industrial Classification (SIC) Manual (1972), department stores are defined as:

> *Retail stores carrying a general line of apparel, such as suits, coats, dresses, accessories; home furnishings, such as table and kitchen appliances, dishes and utensils. These and other merchandise lines are normally arranged in separate sections or departments with the*

*accounting on a departmentalized basis. The store's departments and
functions are integrated under a single management. The stores usually
provide their own charge accounts, deliver merchandise, and maintain
open stocks.*

A few aggregate statistics are sufficient to place the department
store within the context of overall retail trade. One-tenth of all annual
commercial sales in the United States can be attributed to the department store. This is actually quite a large fraction when one considers
the literally millions of retail outlets from individual mom and pop
grocery stores to auto dealerships which populate cities and line
suburban commercial strips. Indeed, if one excludes food stores,
eating and drinking places, building supply outlets, and automotive
dealers from total retail trade, department stores account for nearly a
quarter (23 percent) of all remaining retail sales. Specialty stores that
deal in one line of goods (for example, apparel, furniture, household
appliances, prescription drugs) are responsible for another 29 percent, while variety stores, liquor stores, and mail-order houses make
up an additional 8 percent. Table 1.1 indicates the sales growth in the
industry from 1967 to 1978 (in current dollars). Department stores
have generally held their own.

For stylistic convenience we use the generic term "department
store" to refer to five different modes of retail production and not just
to the segment of the industry which is normally defined as "full-
price, full-line department stores." The five segments, each which
can be described as a "mode of production" of retail services, include:

1. Department store chains.
2. Discount department store chains.
3. Holding companies.
4. Independent department stores.
5. Specialty stores.

Although specialty stores do not meet the criteria set forth in the
SIC definition of department stores, they are discussed in this study
for a number of reasons. Specialty stores gave birth to the conventional and discount department store, and prior to the 1930's they
were the dominant mode of production. Today they are an important
component of the trend toward diversification occurring in the industry as firms within each mode of production develop strategies and
counter-strategies, struggling to increase or maintain their market
share in the face of ever-stiffening competition.

Differences in the structural characteristics and production relations of the various retail modes are described below. Two character-

Table 1.1. U.S. Retail Trade Components

	1967	1970	1971	1972	1973	1974	1975	1976	1977	1978
	Total Sales (Current Dollars) 1967–1978 (Billions)									
Retail Trade, Total	293.0	371.1	410.0	449.1	503.3	536.3	584.8	655.2	724.0	798.8
Retail (excl. food stores, building supplies, auto, and eating and drinking places)	133.0	168.4	183.1	202.1	224.4	244.5	263.3	288.4	314.9	346.4
Department Stores	31.1	38.5	43.1	47.3	52.3	55.0	58.8	64.8	72.3	79.7
Specialty Stores	41.3	51.7	55.4	61.4	68.4	72.8	77.8	85.4	92.0	100.5
Variety Stores, Liquor Stores, Mail-Order	14.6	18.4	19.7	21.2	23.0	24.5	25.8	26.0	27.1	28.5
	Components as a Percentage of Retail									
Department Stores/Total Retail	10.6	10.4	10.5	10.5	10.4	10.3	10.1	9.9	10.0	10.0
Department Stores/Retail (excl.)	24.4	22.9	23.5	23.4	23.3	22.5	22.3	22.5	23.0	23.0
Specialty Stores/Retail (excl.)	31.1	30.7	30.3	30.4	30.5	29.8	29.5	29.6	29.2	29.0
Variety Stores, etc./Retail (excl.)	11.0	10.9	10.8	10.5	10.2	10.0	9.8	9.0	8.6	8.2

SOURCE: U.S. Bureau of the Census, *Monthly Retail Trade Reports* and *Survey of Current Business* (May 1979).

istics should be kept in mind as primarily important in distinguishing each mode: (1) ownership structure, and (2) the payroll/sales ratio.

Department Store Chains (Examples: Sears and J. C. Penney)

Department store chains are the giants of the industry. In 1975, they controlled 89 percent of all department store sales, excluding sales by discount department stores. Because of their size and buying power, department store chains benefit from significant economies of scale, use varying degrees of centralized management, and incorporate advanced technology in order to coordinate the operations of their nationally dispersed branch units. Advertising and technology have been used to reduce the mode's dependency on skilled labor. Their payroll/sales ratio is normally within the range of 12 to 14 percent.

Discount Department Store Chains (Examples: Caldor and K-Mart)

In 1965, discount department store chains surpassed in sales volume all of the conventional department stores combined. Their success is partially due to their low-price appeal and the repeal of the fair trade laws which enabled them to compete on the basis of price with conventional department stores. The chains are highly concentrated. Five percent of all discount department store chains were responsible for 58 percent of all discount department store sales volume in 1977. Management of this mode is highly centralized and, more than any other mode, labor dependency is minimized through extensive use of advertising and part-time workers. Advanced technology is rapidly being introduced and as a result the normal payroll/sales ratio is 11–13 percent.

National Holding Companies (Examples: Federated, Allied and Dayton-Hudson)

National holding companies are composed of wholly owned, geographically dispersed retail firms, each maintaining its own local management. The acquisition of established independents is the primary means of holding-company expansion. The national holding company has control over capital allocation for each firm's future expansion. Capital distribution is based on set levels of return on investment. The "production" labor force has been replaced by advertising to a considerable extent and electronic data processing equipment is rapidly being introduced to tighten managerial control over individual stores. There is an increasing shift toward part-time labor and a reduction in commission sales. Nevertheless, the payroll/sales ratio still runs between 16 percent and 25 percent because of the additional managerial and sales labor required for a higher level of service.

Independent Department Stores (Example: Grover-Cronin, Waltham, Massachusetts and J. H. Corcoran & Company, Cambridge, Massachusetts)

Independent department stores are the one mode of production verging on extinction as a result of business failure or acquisition by holding companies. Independent department stores are usually family operated and locally managed. They have neither the capital base for expansion nor significant scale economies. With increasing competition independents are shifting to a part-time labor force to reduce costs. In-house electronic data processing is usually not affordable by independents nor does their small size necessarily require it. The total payroll/sales ratio is estimated to be between 18 and 22 percent.

Specialty Stores (Examples: Apparel boutiques and discount specialty stores)

Traditionally, specialty stores have been locally managed small shops, selling a narrow range of full-price, high-quality merchandise. This is the most labor-intensive mode, with highly trained sales staff who offer personal service. Other modes have adopted the specialty store concept to expand merchandise lines and develop discount specialty store chains. As department store and discount department store chains as well as holding companies come to control specialty stores, a dependence on technology has developed for the efficient control of individual units within the company as a whole. Payroll/sales ratios range from 16 to 27 percent, depending on the particular mode of operation.

At one time individual corporations operated within only one mode of production. However, the competitive struggle for survival and market dominance has resulted in concentrated ownership within the industry and in many cases different modes of production now operate under one corporate umbrella.

Methodology of the Study

It became clear at the outset of our research that no comprehensive analysis of the department store industry had ever been undertaken. We were able to find fascinating anecdotal histories of particular firms or groups of firms, generally focusing on the personalities and managerial styles of the families who founded and ran them. There was also an abundance of material published in business and trade periodicals, generally more substantive than the anecdotal histories, but still based to a surprising extent on anecdote and on the "received wisdom" of the industry. Carefully reasoned, well-documented articles which were not confined merely to one specific event were the exception rather than the rule. Nevertheless, the articles we discovered allowed us to piece together a picture of an industry in transition.

Once we had formed a set of hypotheses about the structure and behavior of the industry, we proceeded to test what we had learned in a series of interviews with present and former retail industry officials. Our first contact was with a former industry executive, now a professor of management, who shared his impressions, provided us with suggestions and contacts for further interviews, and helped eliminate a few potentially embarrassing misconceptions. For the remainder of our interviews, we chose what we believed would be a broadly representative sample: one independent department store, two regional department stores owned by national holding companies, and three discount department store chains, two of which have their headquarters in New England. (The third chain, originally headquartered in New England, is now bankrupt.) All of the firms except the independent are corporate-owned, multi-unit department stores. We also interviewed at length New England representatives of the Retail Clerks Union, now the United Food and Commercial Workers of America.

Supplementing the secondary source material and the interviews has been our own statistical analysis of two recently available micro data sets. One, kindly made available to us by David Birch of M.I.T., is based on Dun & Bradstreet corporation data for the six New England states. This data set permitted us to trace the births and deaths of department store establishments over the period 1969 to 1976.

The second source was the Longitudinal Employer-Employee Data (LEED) file made available by the U.S. Social Security Administration. This file, used extensively in the chapters on labor mobility and earnings, permitted us to identify the origins and destinations of the highly volatile department store labor force. Computer analysis of LEED told us where the industry's employees are recruited from and where they go when they leave this sector.

Although this is a study of the department store industry throughout the nation, we have chosen at times to focus on the New England region as a source of concrete examples of the industrial transformation we describe. New England was the birthplace of most major innovations in the industry, and the region was the first to reach a high level of retail saturation. Because of its leadership throughout the history of the industry, and for reasons of economy and tractability, we use New England examples in some cases to illustrate national trends. In particular, the data from both LEED and Dun & Bradstreet are for the New England region alone. Nevertheless, our concern with a particular region is intended mainly to illustrate the spatial aspects of the industry's development. The story we tell, based on the histories of department stores in individual regions, is fundamentally a national and even international one.

Endnote

1. U.S. Department of Commerce, *Survey of Current Business* (April 1980).

Chapter 2

A HISTORY AND TAXONOMY OF THE DEPARTMENT STORE INDUSTRY

The early history of the industry laid the groundwork for the industrial transformation we see today. During the 1800's the specialty store was the dominant mode of retailing. In the first two decades of the 20th century, merchants began experimenting with an alternative mode of retailing which would ultimately transform the industry. In order to expand their operations and offer greater convenience to their customers, retailers combined several specialty stores under one roof, and the department store was born.

New England led the nation in this transformation, as it had in the industrial revolution a century earlier. In 1912 Filene's of Boston moved to its present building of eight floors, basement, and subbasement. With this move the store not only nearly doubled the number of selling floors but also expanded its merchandise lines beyond women's wear and accessories. The department store was such a new phenomenon that during the first week alone 715,000 people passed through its doors. The customers of 1912 were dazzled by the enormous store, the large assortment of merchandise, and the experience of going from floor to floor rather than from one specialty shop to another to purchase coordinated apparel. The size of the store, range of merchandise, and services available at Filene's began a revolution in the retail world.

One of the few independent department stores to survive the modern age, Grover-Cronin of Waltham, Massachusetts, provides a vivid example of the transition from specialty shop to department store. In 1928 the store launched a modernization program. The high partitions between individual adjacent specialty shops came down and Grover-Cronin emerged as a full-fledged department store. A greater range of merchandise of excellent quality was available while the service that normally accompanied the small specialty shop was maintained.

The early history of Filene's foreshadowed the future development of the retail industry in two ways. First, the Filene brothers, Lincoln and Edward, visualized retail operations not as a scattering of local individually managed concerns but as nationally consolidated enterprises. In their effort to bring together separate retail establishments, the Filene brothers pioneered national ownership patterns, a far cry from the local sales market of the New England specialty shop and the western general store.

In order to facilitate the exchange between retailers of information formerly regarded as confidential, Lincoln Filene founded the Retail Research Association (RRA) soon after 1916. Major retail stores throughout the country joined the RRA to study problems of merchandising and store operation, and for the first time agreed upon a uniform system of record-keeping. Gradually, the Association recognized the need for collaboration between retailers in buying merchandise, recruiting executives, training employees, improving advertising, and other associated aspects of the retail business. With this expanded purpose in mind, the Association was superceded in 1918 by the formation of the Associated Merchandising Corporation (AMC). As a result of participation in the AMC, Lincoln Filene recognized the need to stabilize earnings through a geographical dispersion of risk and began advocating the formation of a national retail holding company. Eventually Filene's joined with its AMC partners, Abraham & Strauss of Brooklyn, New York, and F. & R. Lazarus & Company of Columbus, Ohio, to form Federated Department Stores. The corporate office of the new holding company, established in Cincinnati, Ohio, allowed each local store autonomous control over sales, but the central office was given the ultimate responsibility for allocating investment funds to the individual stores. Consequently, control over expansion passed from local management to the holding company. This form of "absentee ownership" has come to dominate retailing, particularly as competition and capital requirements increased.

A second way in which the history of Filene's foreshadowed the future of the retail industry was in the development of the "Automatic Bargain Basement," in some ways the precursor of the modern discount department store. As early as 1909, Filene's experimented with the practice of offering brand-name merchandise at discount prices.

The business world expected this radical mode of retailing to fail, but by firmly adhering to their automatic bargain plan, using candid advertising and paying cash for distressed merchandise, Filene's Basement became a spectacular success despite million-dollar losses during its first three years of operation. As is the case today, prices were plainly marked and automatically reduced by a definite percentage on a given day if the goods remained unsold. After 30 days unsold merchandise is donated to charity.

The Automatic Bargain Basement allowed Filene's to broaden its customer base by attracting those who previously could not afford fashion apparel. It tapped an almost guaranteed market and cultivated customer loyalty. Had it not been for the earnings of the Bargain Basement, Filene's would have faced bankruptcy during the Great Depression. Throughout most of the 1930's while the upstairs store operated at a loss, the store's total payroll was met by the Basement's cash sales.

Although three years passed before Filene's Bargain Basement became popular, its success in selling brand-name merchandise at discount prices encouraged other firms to adopt this retailing mode. Unaware of the potential impact of this new concept upon the industry, Filene's had discovered a revolutionary idea that would eventually dominate retailing. Thirty years later full-line discount department stores would capture more of the retail dollar than their traditional full-price brethren.

By the 1950's, purchasing brand-name merchandise for less than list price was no longer a new concept. However, such merchandise was available only to the customer who was willing to do extensive comparative shopping. Through the marketing expertise of retail innovators who foresaw its widespread appeal, the discount concept was successfully applied on a large scale during the 1960's.

As was true for the original department stores, the pioneers of discount outlets were also from New England. The first pipe-rack discount clothing store was Marty's Clothing Mart in South Providence, Rhode Island, founded by Marty Chase, the "grandaddy of all discounting" in 1939. In 1954 "Grandaddy" Chase converted a mill in Cumberland, Rhode Island, and named this new store Ann and Hope. Today it is a large regional discount chain.

Many of the early discount outlets were launched from apparel specialty shops, as were the earlier incarnations of the full-price, full-service department stores. Zayre and Bradlees of Massachusetts were specialty stores which later expanded and emphasized their discount units. A similar pattern was followed by Caldor, which began in 1951 as a one-flight walk-up "hardlines" specialty shop in Port Chester, New York, and moved to Norwalk, Connecticut, in 1958. "Lessees" or private companies which contract with department stores to market a particular line of goods within the store played an important role in expanding the range of merchandise in the pioneer days of mass merchandising. Lessees often ran cosmetic, sporting goods, shoe departments, and "soft goods" sections for companies with hard-line backgrounds.

The first New England full-line discount department store was Arlan's, founded by Lester Palestine in New Bedford, Massachusetts, in 1948. Named after Palestine's daughter, the store originated in a close-out corner of a New Bedford underwear mill. Other retailers followed Arlan's example and New England led the growth of the discount industry in the United States. The majority of discounting pioneers found closed-out mills and factories attractive financially as locations for their new businesses. Kings Department Store came into being in 1949 in an abandoned motorcycle factory in Springfield, Massachusetts. The first Mammoth Mart, founded by Max Coffman, who received his retailing experience in Army-Navy stores, sprang up in an old foundry building in Farmington, Massachusetts, in 1956.

The discounters not only had market appeal, but also benefited from low start-up costs made possible by the widespread availability of vacant buildings which were the remaining shells of New England's dying manufacturing industries. In a limited sense, a revitalization of commerce and community came about with the birth of the discount department store. This novel approach to merchandising provided a new economic base for a small segment of the workforce and the community. The Virginia Dare stores which opened in 1955 in a vacant Fairhaven Mills factory in New Bedford, Massachusetts, and in an old Atlantic Mills textile plant in Providence, Rhode Island, are other examples of how discount stores replaced extinct industry.

Operating on the premise that low mark-ups bring a higher volume of sales, the successful discount store "turns over" merchandise seven to eight times a year, instead of the conventional three to four. By keeping sales costs to a minimum, the early discounters were able to maintain their earnings on slim gross margins*—sometimes as low as 20 to 22 percent. In contrast, full-service, full-price department stores usually maintain 40 to 45 percent margins. In the 1950's and early 1960's, consumer demand was adequate to maintain these high

---

* Gross margin is defined as the difference between merchandise cost and final selling price.

turnover rates and the industry boomed until areas became saturated with discount merchants.

After discounting became a permanent fixture in one segment of the department store industry, food, drug, and conventional department ment stores entered the market. Supermarkets entered discounting by either starting their own discount stores or buying out smaller companies. Recognizing the potential profitability of locating super-market operations near discount outlets, Stop & Shop stores of Boston, Massachusetts, acquired Bradlees in 1961. Also in 1961, the Food Fair chain bought the 33 J.M. Fields stores which had been founded in Salem, Massachusetts, in a converted fabric mill in 1955. Drugstore chains entered discounting by expanding their nonprescription drug units, in some cases becoming full-line discount stores. Drug chains also grew out of existing retail chains. Stop & Shop, having already acquired Bradlees, diversified in 1967, creating a chain of discount priced drugstores called Medi-Mart.

The behavior of the discount retail industry during the 1960's clearly manifests the "grow or die" merchandising philosophy. The almost universal policy was to penetrate every conceivable market in a rush to exclude competitors from choice locations. As a result, the number of discount outlets nationwide grew from a handful in the mid-1950's to 1,329 in 1960 to almost 7,400 in 1977. Sales exploded from $2 billion to $39.2 billion during this same period.[1] By 1965 discount stores had become the number one retailing mode in general merchandising, surpassing full-price department stores with a 9.8 percent share of the market.[2]

The struggle for market share within and between modes of merchandise trade has had profound implications for employment and the fortunes of individual communities. Virulent competition has led to constant innovation aimed at increasing productivity and profitability while the expansion of one mode at the expense of another has altered the pattern of ownership and control in the industry. Meanwhile government regulations have played no small role in determining the overall structure of this sector of the economy.

The transformation in mode dominance from the specialty store to the discount department store has occurred as a result of the nature of competition within the retail industry, as well as changing government policies and a variety of economic and demographic factors. In order to better understand the influence of each of these on the restructuring of the retail industry the following section provides a description of the ownership patterns, management structures, merchandise lines, consumer markets, sales strategies, and labor force characteristics which are associated with each mode of retail trade.

Modes of Retail Trade: A Taxonomy

At one time, ownership patterns were such that firms confined themselves to operations in a single mode, but since the early sixties, ownership has become diversified. For example, one holding company, Federated, owns Filene's, Abraham & Strauss, and Bloomingdale's—all full-service department stores—but also owns and operates Gold Circle, Gold Triangle, and Gold Key stores—all discount chains. Zayre has diversified from the discount mode into the specialty store industry with its Hit Or Miss and T.J. Maxx Shops. The merging of modes is a result of increased competition and a desire on the part of retailers to preserve and increase their share of the market. Each mode still maintains its own distinct set of production relations and structural characteristics, although these are sometimes modified as the industry evolves. The appearance of the "specialty store chain" is an example of the transformation taking place in the industry.

Department Store Chains

Three forms of retail trade have supplanted the independent department store since World War II: the department store chain (defined as a corporation with eleven or more units), the discount department store, and the national retail holding company. By 1975 sales from the first two of these accounted for 89 percent of all department store sales, leaving independents and holding companies with only eleven percent of the market. The best-known examples of full-service department store chains are Sears, J.C. Penney, and Montgomery-Ward, which in 1975 were the first, second, and sixth largest general merchandise retailers in the United States. In 1973 these three alone accounted for $22.6 billion of sales or 43 percent of all department store sales in the United States.[3]

A department store chain expands by building its own branch units, each of which is a near "clone" of the original and carries essentially the same merchandise packaged and sold in the same way. The department store chain differs from the discount chain in both its merchandise price range and its level of customer service.

Although Sears is the largest marketer of general merchandise in the world, with $14.95 billion in sales in 1976 and $17.22 billion in 1977, it is not atypical of large chains. Begun in 1895 as a mail-order business, Sears began selling over-the-counter only in 1925 as a response to growing urbanization, the widespread use of the auto-mobile, and the decline in mail-order sales. The first retail outlets, like those of its competitors, were located in the downtown areas of cities with populations of at least 100,000. After World War II Sears followed the population shift to the suburbs, but continued to maintain many of its downtown stores. By 1976 Sears had 859 retail outlets averaging 129,000 square feet each, plus 2,920 other sales facilities and independent catalog merchants. Of Sears' total 1976 revenue, 80.9 percent came through its retail outlets, 9.6 percent through mail-order, and 9.5 percent through industrial sales, repair services, and finance charges.[4] After taxes it earned an 11.7 percent return on investment (ROI), a rate of return which is approximately equal to the average for the largest 32 general merchandisers in the country.[5] In the last two years Sears' retailing profits have shown a downward trend as changes in merchandising strategies have proven unsuccess-ful. Its merchandising management has been reorganized to give headquarters tighter control of operations.

As the giants of the industry, the large department store chains—if well managed—have the power to own or control all facets of the retail business. In the early years of the department store chain, some companies such as Sears and Wards adopted a defensive strategy of vertical integration by acquiring financial control of their merchan-dise suppliers. The stated objective was to ensure an adequate supply of goods at a reasonable price. As early as 1948 Sears owned or held partial interest in thirty manufacturing companies.

Whether large department store chains own the manufacturer or not, they are capable of exerting a high degree of control over many of their suppliers, or what the industry calls "resources," simply through their ability to purchase the lion's share of an individual manufacturer's output. Manufacturers produce merchandise to the specifications of large chains because chains have the finances to buy in large quantities. For example, in the clothing line, Sears has a fashion coordinator who works with leading designers to select colors and styles for each particular season. Children's wear sources are controlled even more directly. One buyer is responsible for purchas-ing fabrics at quantity discounts and having them dyed and shipped to Sears' sources for manufacture into finished garments.

This control over manufacturers and vendors increases the ability of department store chains to generate capital resources, further enabling them to undertake risk and ride out market fluctuations. The opposite is true for smaller retailers. The extent of control and price leverage a retailer has over the manufacturer is dependent on its size and capital base.

The department store chain's consumer market spans a broad range of income and social class. While most department stores primarily feature soft lines and women's apparel, department store chains normally carry a full range of "brown" and "white" goods in addition to apparel and accessories. "Brown goods" include stereos, televisions, and radios. "White goods" are the larger kitchen and laundry consumer durables—refrigerators, washers, dryers, etc. Sears and Wards originally concentrated on the hard lines including furniture, hardware, tools, guns, fishing tackle, and the durable goods created by the development of the automobile and consumer appliances: tires, batteries, and other auto accessories, refrigerators, and washing machines. In earlier days, "Sears . . . gave its store appeal to the man—the family—the home—the car—and relatively little appeal to style."[6] Over the past fifteen years, however, the major department store chains have attempted to appeal to all family members and thus compete with the regular department store and in some cases even with the specialty shop.

Organizations as complex as the large department store chains are constantly struggling to evolve management structures which maximize profit and ensure survival. In this sense, as one retail expert maintains, any large department store chain confronts "management problems similar to those which DuPont, General Motors, and Jersey Standard . . . [confront] and for much the same reason."[7] Since 1915 Sears has been through three major managerial reorganizations in an attempt to strike the proper balance between local territorial control and its central office authority. Since Sears penetrates virtually every region of the country and tries to appeal to families covering nearly the full range of the income distribution, central management has been forced to rely to a great extent on the knowledge of individual local, zone and territorial managers. However, basic control over capital flows—which territories are permitted to expand and which are forced to contract—remains firmly entrenched as the prerogative of central management. These decisions are based almost exclusively on return on investment (ROI) targets for existing outlets. At Sears, the residual income approach is used to measure store performance. Under this approach an amount of interest is calculated by multiplying the amount of assets employed by the store by an established interest rate set by the Chicago home office. This interest is then deducted from the store profits to yield the residual income. The rate of interest is based on the cost of capital.

The depression of the 1930's played a significant role in bringing about centralization of supervision and the control of the retail stores and mail-order plants. Increased centralization appears to occur within all department store chains when sales lag or profit rates decline. To accomplish the complex task of controlling operations at many different locations, the large department store chains have been the pioneers in adapting electronic data processing (EDP). The most advanced lightpen point-of-sale inventory systems have been introduced, and banks of computers in the central office are capable of monitoring sales, profits, and inventories for each outlet. The sheer sales volume of the chains has made EDP necessary, while the level of assets and profits has made it commercially feasible.

For advertising the large chains use the full range of media, from seasonal catalogues to daily newspaper advertisements and radio and television. Unlike the specialty store and the smaller independent, the department store chain relies on advertising to sell the product, leaving the "sales staff" to process orders. Advertising has become the chief means of reducing the skills required of the retail sales force, while EDP has eliminated most of the manual inventory and accounting tasks. For the most part, elimination of the well-trained knowledgeable sales person has allowed the department store chain to convert much of its workforce to a part-time basis, so that as many as 70 percent or more of employees work less than a full schedule. All of this maintains the payroll-to-sales ratio within the 12 to 14 percent range. With this low ratio, the department store chain is capable of underpricing even the most cost-conscious independent.

Discount Department Store Chains

As late as the mid-1950's, the discount department store posed no threat to the full-service independent, the department store chains, or holding company acquisitions. They were few, their merchandise range was narrow, and they possessed little customer appeal. Yet by 1965 the discounters were able to surpass in sales volume all of the conventional mode department stores combined (see Table 2.1). Their success ultimately lies in their low-overhead, low-price policy which appeals to an increasing number of price-conscious consumers. Due to the repeal of fair-trade legislation, the discounter has pro-

Table 2.1.   Sales Volume by Retail Trade Mode (Current Dollars), 1960–1977

Year	Discounters[a] Sales Volume (in billions of dollars)	Percentage of Total General Merchandise Sales	Department Stores[a] Sales Volume (in billions of dollars)	Percentage of Total General Merchandise Sales
1960	2.0	—	—	—
1961	3.5	—	—	—
1962	6.9	—	—	—
1963	9.3	—	—	—
1964	10.8	9.8	14.3	13.0
1965	13.2	9.8	12.7	9.4
1966	15.0	9.5	13.4	8.5
1967	16.6	10.0	14.1	8.6
1968	19.4	11.0*	15.1*	8.7*
1969	22.2	12.0	16.0	8.7
1970	24.4	12.5	16.0	8.2
1971	26.6	12.8	17.5	8.4
1972	29.0	12.6	20.3	8.8
1973	29.9	11.9	22.3	8.8
1974	31.4	11.4	23.9	8.7
1975	32.9	10.9	26.2	8.7
1976	36.1	11.0	30.0	9.2
1977	39.2	10.7	32.1	8.8

SOURCE: "True Look at the Discount Industry," *Discount Merchandiser* (May 1960–1977).

* Estimates.
[a] Excludes mail-order and other nonretail outlet sales of department stores.
— Information Unavailable.

vided increasing competition to the moderate price, conventional department store in brand-name products.

There are two types of discount chains. The first type is regional and includes such firms as Caldor, headquartered in Norwalk, Connecticut, and Bradlee's in Boston. The strategy of these chains has been to restrict their market penetration to a single region and blanket that area so as to spread the fixed costs of warehousing, management, and advertising. The second type of chain is national, and includes such firms as K-Mart, Woolco, Kings, and Gold Circle. K-Mart, headquartered in Detroit, Michigan, is regarded as retailing's *tour de force*. In 1976, it added more than one new store every working day—271 in all—to its existing 1,254 outlets spread across the country, in Puerto Rico, Canada, and Australia. In the United States, the firm is operating stores in 256 out of the 275 standard metropolitan statistical areas, and is continuing to grow. By 1981 K-Mart plans to open 1,000 more stores, many of which will presumably compete with veteran regional chains.[8] In the process it will no doubt drive many of its weaker competitors into bankruptcy. Its massive size also allows it to reap quantity discounts from vendors, something which independents and smaller chains cannot do.

While other chains are not as large as K-Mart, the industry is increasingly dominated by big operators. Five percent of all discount firms, those with 50 or more units, were responsible for 58 percent of all discount department store sales volume in 1977. These 31 firms operated 61 percent of the more than 7,300 discount outlets throughout the United States (see Figure 2.1 and Table 2.2).

Discount chain store management is highly centralized, particularly as each unit is an almost perfect clone of the others in the chain. Little discretion is left to the local store manager even in the area of display. One chain actually sends color photographs of the proper position of displays for every section of each store and requires local managers to set up their own stores to mirror the photographs. Wage and hiring policy, investment, expansion, and contraction are all determined in the home office and communicated to the local management.

In the early discount era, the product line was limited by available capital and by fair-trade laws. Firms were restricted to the soft lines which required smaller inventory investment and returned higher overall margins. Fair-trade laws allowed manufacturers to limit the supply of their merchandise to firms charging the manufacturer's suggested retail price. This excluded discounters who were then forced to carry products with unfamiliar labels and of unknown quality. As these laws were repealed in one state after another, the discount merchants were able to expand their product lines, and with this the target customer population broadened. Today discount chains draw from all segments of the income distribution and particularly from middle class suburban families. In 1967 a Cleveland Press Survey reported that since most discount stores were located in suburban shopping areas, it was not surprising that discounters were less frequently patronized by low-income families. With inflation, the percentage has undoubtedly increased. As a late entrant to the retail industry, and because of its low overhead requirement, the overwhelming majority of discount outlets are in suburban locations on low-cost land.

More than any other mode, the discount segment of the industry minimizes labor dependency. Its 11–13 percent payroll/sales ratio is obtained by using part-time, less-skilled workers tied to an advertising intensive sales strategy. It utilizes all forms of media, but relies

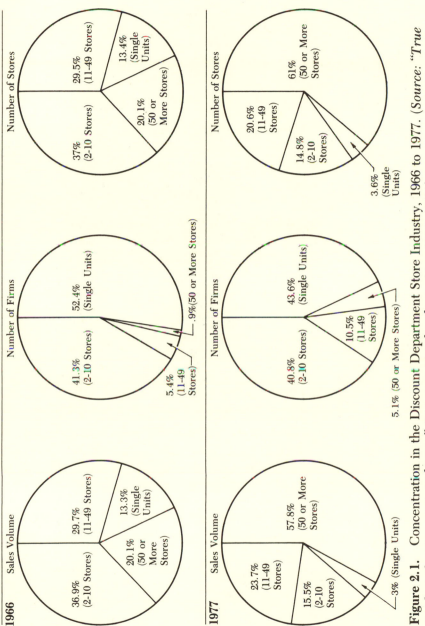

Figure 2.1. Concentration in the Discount Department Store Industry, 1966 to 1977. (*Source:* "True Look at the Discount Industry," Discount Merchandiser, *May 1966–1977.*)

Table 2.2.   The Size Distribution of Discount Department Store Chains, 1966–1977

Size of Company	1966			1970			1974			1977		
	Sales Volume (millions of dollars)	No. of Firms	No. of Stores	Sales Volume (millions of dollars)	No. of Firms	No. of Stores	Sales Volume (millions of dollars)	No. of Firms	No. of Stores	Sales Volume (millions of dollars)	No. of Firms	No. of Stores
Single Units	1,997	469	469	2,580	456	456	2,104	458	458	1,176	266	266
2–3 Stores	2,252	227	526	2,875	222	543	2,594	234	564	1,568	126	303
4–10 Stores	3,287	141	770	4,795	133	735	4,047	140	826	4,509	123	787
11–25 Stores	2,597	37	602	3,979	48	832	4,148	50	799	4,078	42	672
26–49 Stores	1,861	12	432	3,436	14	845	4,851	26	933	5,215	22	844
50 Stores or more	3,017	8	704	6,693	25	1,647	13,681	24	2,715	22,664	31	4,491
Total	15,011	895	3,503	24,357	898	5,058	31,426	932	6,295	39,211	610	7,363

SOURCE: "True Look at the Discount Industry," *Discount Merchandiser* (May 1966–1977).

particularly on local newspapers and area television. Electronic data processing is rapidly taking over, especially among the larger chains.

The soaring growth pattern of the discount general merchandise industry has brought periodic stages of over-expansion combined with under-capitalization. In each cycle there is initially zealous expansion, followed by a shake-out period in which smaller and/or weaker stores are liquidated or acquired by other chains. The latest cycle of consolidation occurred in 1977 when the total number of discount firms declined from 741 to 610. Single-store proprietorships and those firms with two to three outlets suffered the greatest mortality.[9]

Perhaps the real danger facing discount stores over the next decade will be the erosion of their competitive margins. As early as 1972, studies reported in the trade magazine *Discount Store News* suggested that in some departments the discounters' initial markup had increased to only five or six points below that of conventional department stores.[10] In the future the difference between discount store and conventional department store prices may become even slimmer, but for the present the discount chain continues to lead the price competition.

The National Holding Company

A retail holding company is an enterprise composed of wholly owned, geographically dispersed retail firms, each of which maintains its own customer identity and local management. The chief operating officers for each firm, appointed by the holding company, are responsible for the day-to-day operations of each outlet, while the central authority retains full allocative control over all capital resource allocation.

The best-known national retail holding companies are Federated Department Stores, Allied Stores Corporation, May Department Stores Company, and Dayton-Hudson Corporation. In 1977 these four combined had 807 retail outlets and total sales in excess of $11.4 billion, more than $2 billion more than the whole J.C. Penney chain with its 1,686 stores nationwide.[11]

The growth pattern of the typical holding company can be illustrated by the corporate acquisition history of the May Company, the first of these to be established. In 1910 it acquired and began operating the Schoenberg Mercantile Company of St. Louis, Missouri (parent of the Famous Department Store founded in 1869), the May Shoe & Clothing Company of Denver, Colorado, and the May Company of Cleveland, Ohio. Subsequently it acquired Wm. Barr Dry

Goods Company (St. Louis, Missouri, 1911), Boggs and Buhl Company (Pittsburgh, Pennsylvania, 1912), M. O'Neil Company (Akron, Ohio, 1912), Hamberger & Sons (Los Angeles, California, 1923), Bernheimer-Leader Stores (Baltimore, Maryland, 1932), Kaufmann Department Stores (Pittsburgh, Pennsylvania, 1946), the Strauss-Hirshberg Company (Youngstown; Warren, Ohio, 1948), and the T.S. Martin Company (Sioux City, Iowa, 1949). During the 1950's it continued its rapid expansion program by acquiring the Spring-Holzworth store in Alliance, Ohio; the Sharon Store in Sharon, Pennsylvania; Enlanger Dry Goods Company in Canton, Ohio; and Davids & Fisher Stores in Denver, Colorado. In 1959 it merged with the Hecht Company of Baltimore, Maryland. One of the May Company's biggest postmerger acquisitions was G. Fox & Company of Hartford, Connecticut, consummated in November 1965. At the time of its purchase, G. Fox had been a family-run independent for nearly 120 years.

The May Company entered the discount store field in 1969 when it formed Venture Stores, Inc. This division was expanded in 1978 when it acquired 19 Turnstyle outlets from the Jewel Company. With this broadened capital base, May Company has been able to expand into the supermarket industry and has acquired purchasing and merchandising corporations in England and Hong Kong. In all, this one holding company operates 234 department stores organized into 15 chains across the country.

The histories of Allied, Federated, and Dayton-Hudson are similar. Incorporated in 1928 with 27 wholly owned department stores, Allied Stores now operates 7 regional shopping centers, 164 department stores, and 10 discount outlets spread across the country from Boston to Tacoma and Grand Rapids to Miami. Among its holdings are the Jordan Marsh stores of Boston, Read's of Connecticut, Levy's of Savannah, Georgia, and Bon Marche stores in the Northwestern states. Federated, incorporated one year later, was a consolidation of three existing smaller holding companies which today contain some of the most prestigious department store names in retail marketing: Abraham & Strauss, Bloomingdale's, the Boston Store, Bullock's, Burdine's, Filene's, Foley's, Goldsmith's, Lazarus, Levy's, and I. Magnin & Company. Like Allied and the May Company, Federated has also jumped into the discount chain business through its Gold Circle, Gold Triangle, and Gold Key outlets. All told, it has 223 department and discount stores and 82 Ralph's supermarkets.

The last of the "Big Four" is Dayton-Hudson, one of the more recently developed retail holding companies. First listed in *Fair-*

child's Manual in 1966 with $220 million in sales, today it is the eighth largest general merchandise retailer in the United States, with sales of $2.2 billion in 1977. Its growth can be attributed to its acquisition of Lechmere Sales Company of Boston and J. E. Caldwell Company of Philadelphia in March 1969, followed two months later by its merger with the J.L. Hudson Company of Detroit. It now operates 31 full-service department stores, 59 Target Discount outlets, 4 Lechmere stores, and numerous specialty shops that deal in jewelry, books, and consumer electronics.[12]

In addition to opening new branch stores, holding companies expand by acquiring established independents. This expansion strategy distinguishes the holding company from a department store chain. The independent is often a willing partner in these arrangements for a number of reasons. One is that the owner family may no longer wish to be responsible for management. Another is the desire of the original owners to take advantage of the scale economies afforded the individual units of the parent company. The most important reason, however, is related to capital requirements. The typical family-run independent generates inadequate retained earnings for physical expansion or renovation and often finds it difficult to successfully preserve its share of the market. Absorption into a holding company is often accompanied by a promise to extend investment resources to the local management of the new acquisition. Absorption or merger thus becomes the means to survive in a competitive market.

For the most part, the individual firms within the large holding company promote brand-names rather than their own store label. In doing this they generally use both the print and electronic media for advertising. Here they benefit from co-op programs where the manufacturer shares advertising costs, often on a 50/50 basis, with the individual retailer. This provides heavily subsidized advertising not usually available to the smaller independent or the department store chain which sells its own store-name products.

The labor force in the holding company is similar to that found in the department store chains. Advertising, rather than the salesperson, is used to convince the customer to buy, and EDP is rapidly being implemented to reduce inventory costs and to keep tighter managerial control over individual store units. The result is an increasing shift toward part-time employees and a reduction in commission sales. Overall the payroll/sales ratio runs from 16–20 percent in the regular full-price department stores (for example, Filene's) to as much as 23–25 percent in the higher price/higher service stores such as Bloomingdale's.

The Independent Department Store

The one mode of production which is bordering on extinction, the independent department store, is being squeezed out of the market from all sides—by the new specialty shops, the department store chains, and of course the discount retailer.

Many independents were started over a century ago and descendants of the original founders have traditionally been the parties responsible for carrying the store through the turbulent changes in the current retail environment. The founding family often owns 95 percent or more of the store's assets, permitting in-house managerial decisions and personal attention to the survival of the firm. Unlike other modes, many of the independents that survive on their own espouse a "break-even" attitude rather than the "grow-or-die" philosophy which is characteristic of corporate structured retailers.

More than any other mode of production, the independent relies on advertising and location for its survival. One particular local Massachusetts store spends approximately 3.5 percent of its sales dollar on advertising (a full percentage point more than the average corporate department store) because it cannot spread advertising expenditures over many outlets. To counteract the financial drain, this retailer designs and prints all of its advertisements in-house. It has its own print shop which allows flexibility and minimizes the cost of commercial work.

The location of a store is especially important to insure a constant flow of business. One surviving independent is located in the "heart" of a small city, at the intersection of several major highways, making the store accessible from all directions. To accommodate its customers, this store has a large parking area, a critical convenience for any downtown location. The absence of strategic location and ample parking facilities is a serious contributing factor to the demise of many of these one-unit stores.

Independents most often sell brand-name merchandise in the middle and upper-middle price range although some have diversified into the discount business through a basement department or "downstairs store." This may have been primarily a defensive maneuver to hold its own against the discounter's threat of lower prices for brand-name merchandise, but it also broadens the store's customer base and merchandise appeal.

Although there are no concrete data available, it appears that profit rates among independents lag behind those in other modes of trade. This may be due partly to higher average fixed costs per sales dollar and partly to higher investment cost as a result of a restricted range of finance options. Holding companies and retail chains finance expansion in large measure through retained earnings or money borrowed at or close to prime rate. Independents and specialty stores usually have insufficient retained earnings and do not have the same favored status in capital markets.

Independents usually operate out of one large downtown store with anywhere from 175,000 to 300,000 or more square feet. Until recently the number of regular full-time employees exceeded part-time, but with increased competition it has become necessary to extend business hours into the evening and reduce, where possible, the cost of employee benefits. This action has caused a shift toward a larger part-time workforce which works peak hour shifts and does not enjoy the same fringe benefit structure as full-time staff. One New England independent reported that 75 percent of its total 400 employees work part-time. For the Christmas rush, this firm hires an additional 600 sales workers on a part-time basis. As with the specialty shop, there is an attempt to train the full-time workforce to offer credible sales assistance and gain some merchandise knowledge. This is done through limited classroom instruction and more extensive on-the-job training. The total payroll-to-sales ratio is estimated to be between 18 and 22 percent.

As in the case of the specialty store, the newest forms of electronic data processing are beyond the financial means of most independents. Payroll functions may be subcontracted to firms that specialize in this service, but, due to their size, most independents continue using manual record and inventory procedures. The few survivors that have not yet been forced to liquidate or succumb to an acquisition bid do so because of excellent management overcoming the multiple disadvantages of downtown location, sub-optimal size, inadequate capital, and the growing competition from other retail modes. In most cases pride of ownership in this last vestige of *petite bourgeoisie* capital is necessary to offset the lower profitability that accompanies its mode of operation.

The Specialty Store

Specialty stores have traditionally been small shops, each retailing a narrow line of full-priced, high-quality merchandise. By definition they are not department stores, but they are the major form of competition for other general merchandise modes. Examples range from the high-fashion apparel boutique to record and hardware stores. They are geared toward consumers who are willing to pay higher prices for merchandise in order to obtain somewhat more service and in some cases a more complete line of goods. An independent specialty store usually has local ownership and management, the owner often being the manager and frequently also a member of the sales staff. The owner of a successful specialty store has traditionally invested personal effort in building a regular clientele and in knowing his/her customers by name, tastes, and interests.

Consequently, managers prefer to hire sales personnel who have had previous sales experience or who present a personal style which fits the store's image. In most cases, the employees are trained on the job according to a strict curriculum covering customer service, merchandise promotion, and product quality. For this reason, the specialty store is the most labor-intensive mode of retail production with an estimated total payroll-to-sales ratio ranging from 23 to 27 percent, according to one industry source. Many employees work full-time with the intent of making the job a career, and may progress from sales to management positions. Some use their experience to begin their own stores. This emphasis placed on personal service generates the regular clientele that a specialty store depends on for survival.

Specialty outlets are predominantly located in the central city, where they depend on the amount of foot traffic in the shopping district to increase sales. In the past decade specialty shops have increasingly located in suburban shopping malls. Their target customers often live in suburbia and the "anchor stores" (main stores in the mall) bring in the needed pedestrian traffic. A specialty store's main source of advertisement is the front window display, which may cost the store between $100 and $500 a week if professionally done.

The intensified market competition between conventional and discount department stores has forced each of these modes to look for alternative strategies to preserve or increase its market share. As a result, two variations of the traditional form of specialty shop ownership have developed. One is the use of the specialty mode by the discount department store chain to maintain its low price but carry a quality of merchandise not usually associated with the discount mode. Similarly, the regular department store can use the discount specialty mode to capitalize on the price advantage uncharacteristic of its traditional role, yet still maintain its public image as a source of quality merchandise. The amount of personal service and management of a discount specialty store depends largely on whether a firm is stressing the "specialty" or "discount" aspects of the trade.

The discount specialty store, which was developed as a means of increasing a firm's competitive advantage, has further intensified the rivalry between the conventional and discount department modes. The differences between them have become less distinct as the newer discount specialty stores increasingly become units within large chains associated with even larger merchandising corporations.

Still another form of the specialty shop has developed as the conventional chain store has made further use of the departmental concept for internal expansion. Within the traditional store, the customer can now find a group of shops specializing, for example, in men's dress wear or home furnishings. Filene's of Boston is currently expanding in this manner.

Electronic data processing and other forms of advanced technology are not necessary in an individual specialty store or small chain and are usually not affordable. Inventory control and tagging is done manually and is often a productive activity because sales personnel become familiar with the store merchandise. In contrast, the new large specialty store chains, especially those owned by a holding company, are dependent upon EDP in order to efficiently control inventory, coordinate the buying and selling activities of individual units in the chain, and maintain performance records on each store. The substantial initial fixed costs of EDP are spread among the individual units of the chain.

The Struggle Between Modes of Retail Trade

A summary of the structural characteristics of the five retail trade modes is found in Table 2.3. Structural differences reflect the strategies employed by each mode to maintain or increase its market share in the face of heightened inter- and intra-mode competition.

In the escalating struggle between modes there have been periods of over-expansion and cyclical "shake-outs" within the industry. The Chairman of the Board of S.S. Kresge Company commented in a speech before the Seattle Rotary Club: "The laws of supply and demand and survival of the fittest work in their most elemental forms in retailing. Thousands of new retailing ventures are started every year, and almost an equal number fail. Our industry is in a constant state of ferment, and competition is recognized as being more virulent in retailing than in any other major branch of American industry."[13]

The most significant development in the recent history of competition in the industry is the dramatic rise of the discount department

Table 2.3. Modes of Production in the Department Store Industry—Operations, Control, and Structure

Locus of Management Decisions	Department Store Chain	Discount Department Store Chain	Holding Company	Independent Department Store	Specialty Store
Day-To-Day Operations	Local/Central	Central	Local	Local	Local
Investment Decisions	Central	Central	Central	Local	Local
Location	Central City/ Suburban Mall	Suburbs	Central City/ Suburban Mall	Central City	Central City/ Suburban Mall
Production Lines	Full-Line	Full-Line	Full-Line	Soft Goods Concentration Hard Goods	Single Specialty Hard or Soft Goods
Target Customer Market	Middle Income	All	Middle to Upper Income	All	Middle to Upper Income
Types of Advertising	All Media	Circulars/ All Media	All Media/Co-op	Circulars	Window/Fashion Shows
Labor Force Skills	Skilled/Unskilled	Unskilled	Skilled/Unskilled	Skilled/Unskilled	Skilled
Part-Time vs. Full-Time	70/30	80/20	60/40	70/30	Full-Time Majority
Use of EDP	Full	Full	Full	No	No
Payroll/Sales Ratio	12–14%	11–13%	16–25%	18–22%	16–27%

store. Since the early 1960's, two seemingly contradictory trends have dominated the retail industry. Consumers have "traded up," expressing their desire for better merchandise and service and their willingness to pay for them. Simultaneously, a large proportion of the consumer market has turned to the discount sector. The phenomenal growth of the discounters provides convincing evidence that the discount formula—price appeal, suburban location, and longer store hours—holds a basic attraction for a large number of families.

With its growth, the discount industry has suffered wrenching "shake-out" periods. As one industry source noted, betting on their discount formula some discount retailers attempt to build highly leveraged capital empires. In doing so, some chains expand well beyond their capital resources. Given the narrow margins in the industry, a dip in aggregate demand, inattention to the cost side, or increased competition forces a credit crunch. In such cases, many firms fail, and not always the smallest.

Many retailers, especially those in well-financed and managed stores, take the attitude that the shake-out cycle is beneficial to the industry as a whole. They maintain that the retail industry should operate according to the law of survival of the fittest. The president of the Interstate Discount Department Store chain, which had over $700 million in sales in 1971, asserted:[14]

> *The discount industry will move on to a new and higher level of acceptance as the public becomes aware that the bankruptcies and credit problems apply to the small, marginal, and unimportant companies which have no place in the industry and ultimately will be weeded out.*

The Chairman of Arlan's Department Store (1969 sales—$363 million) echoed these sentiments: "Some of the weak, poorly managed companies will probably get hurt, but then, they always do."[15]

Ironically, both of these companies, despite their size and bravado, filed for bankruptcy under Chapter XI in 1972. But it was not until 1975, when W.T. Grant, the retailing giant, went bankrupt with 1,069 stores and debts exceeding $1 billion,[16] that all retailers and—importantly—all banks realized that no firm, regardless of size, is invulnerable. Size alone does not guarantee longevity.

The growth of discounting in the retail industry has brought about a heightened struggle for power and dominance among the modes. Discounters have created an enormous challenge to the conventional department store and as a result have redefined the retail world. This has been accomplished by the following means:

1. Forcing traditional prices down and pressuring conventional stores to shorten their margins.
2. Expanding the market for brand name goods and "creating a high-velocity check-out at retail to match high-velocity assembly lines at the plant."[17]
3. Bringing about the successful challenge of fair trade and Blue Laws in many states.
4. Giving the customer the convenience of late-hour shopping.
5. Equalizing markets by moving cosmopolitan styles within the reach of all customers.

Once conventional department stores, department store chains, and holding companies realized the challenge posed by the discount chains, they moved quickly to diversify their capital base. In an attempt to preserve their market share, they exploited new enterprises, some akin to but others distinctly different from their traditional department store activities. Investment funds were redirected during the late 1960's and early 1970's toward food service units, drug chains, auto service centers, book store chains, shopping center construction, and the creation of management credit and loan companies. Some firms sank capital into realty development and mutual funds, while others expanded into insurance. Sears' Allstate home and auto insurance business, first begun in 1931, has been substantially expanded; by 1976 it contributed a full 25 percent to the parent company's pre-tax profits.[18]

Other traditional retailers followed the ageless maxim, "If you can't beat 'em, join 'em." They diverted capital resources to the construction or acquisition of discount department store chains. Federated has three such outlets (Gold Circle, Gold Triangle, and Gold Key), Allied has two (Almart and J.B. Hunter), Dayton-Hudson owns Lechmere Sales, and J.C. Penney opened its Treasury chain in 1969. In this way the holding company and the department store chain could compete directly in the discount sector. Federated's shift in strategy was in partial response to the Federal Trade Commission's ruling prohibiting Federated from acquiring another department store for five years after it purchased Bullock's of California in the mid-1960's. Similarly, some independents like Grover-Cronin opened bargain basements.

At the other end of the spectrum, a second strategy evolved to preserve market share. Some department stores (as well as some discount department store chains) traded up to take advantage of increased consumer affluence. In the 1950's specialty stores had been the chief victims of the continued growth of the other retail modes. As a result of the repeal of fair-trade legislation (detailed in Chapter 7) and the consequent shift of basic merchandise lines from department stores to discounters, conventional department stores, in an attempt to fill the vacated square footage, began leasing departments within their stores to specialty shops. The new specialty departments—each with its own motif—provided a high level of personal service, a new retail image for the conventional department store, and appeal to the fashion-conscious consumer.

Leasing introduced a new role for the victims of the 1950's competition. Specialty stores were now protected from failure by merging with the financial power of the department store. This new trend also gave the specialty store access to the suburban market, where it became a vital part of a growing number of suburban malls.

In addition to initial leasing, there was also acquisition of specialty store chains. Ann Taylor was purchased by Garfinkels of New York and The Lodge was acquired by C. W. Brunhenmeyer of the Netherlands, which had previously acquired Orbach's of New York City. The discount department store chains also utilized the specialty store mode to increase their market share.

The "image" of a specialty shop provides the department store with a vital weapon in the retail battle. Bloomingdale's, Lord & Taylor, and Macy's stress their personalized image which is then carried into their branch stores. If image has become nearly as important as the merchandise, it may be because most of the major stores offer nearly identical product lines. No store has an "exclusive" on big-volume designers anymore and the critical variable has become presentation. If a retailer knows exactly who his customer is and how to present the merchandise, that store has a competitive edge. This diversification phenomenon has indeed permitted the traditional retail sector to recover some of its previous market share. This trend has made specialty stores one of the fastest growing segments in the retail industry.

Traditional independent department stores, department store chains, and holding companies had at one time over 20 percent of all U.S. retail trade, including food items. By 1964 discounters had captured 9.8 percent of the total retail market, while the share of traditional general merchandisers had shrunk to 13 percent. Six years later, with the continuing explosive expansion of the discount department store chains, the conventional retail sector had slipped to 8.2

percent of the total market. Since that time the counter-offensive waged by the traditional general merchandiser has allowed this sector to recoup some of its loss.[19]

The struggle between retail modes has now intensified, particularly in the Northeast where consumer markets are rapidly becoming saturated. (The concept of market "saturation" is explored in Chapter 3.) A new strategy by one mode is quickly countered by another (if capital resources permit) in an attempt to preserve or expand market share. And increasingly the battle is not simply between modes, but within them as individual firms struggle for dominance. The struggle is further expanded by capital-intensive conglomeration as illustrated by the Mobil acquisition of Montgomery-Ward in 1976. This heightened competitive struggle—of strategy met by counter-strategy—lies at the root of the always frenetic retail industry.

The strategies employed by each mode in competing for market dominance have therefore played a major role in shaping the retail industry. It is the very nature of retail competition which has led to constant innovation in management structures, sales strategies, and overall ownership patterns. The resulting differences in the production relations and structural characteristics of each mode have been determined by this struggle but also, in part, by a variety of economic and demographic factors. These broader macroeconomic variables, to which we now turn, determine the overall health of the industry.

Endnotes

1. "The True Look of the Discount Industry," *Discount Merchandiser* (May 1960–1977).
2. *Ibid*. (May 1965), p. 36.
3. Calculated from data in *Fairchild's Financial Manual of Retail Stores,* 1974, and *Department Store Retailing in an Era of Change* (Washington: U.S. Department of Commerce, June 1975), p. 5.
4. Vijayaraghavan Govindarajan, "Sears Roebuck and Company: A Historical Background" (Boston, Mass: Harvard Business School, Intercollegiate Case Clearing House, No. 4-179-123 rev. 2/79), p. 1, 3.
5. *Fairchild's Financial Manual of Retail Stores* (1979).
6. Alfred D. Chandler, *Strategy and Structure* (Cambridge, Mass.: MIT Press, 1962), p. 236.
7. *Ibid.*, p. 225.
8. *Discount Merchandiser* (June 1978), p. 146.
9. *Ibid*. (May 1978).
10. "70's—A Decade for Individuality," *Discount Store News* (December 11, 1972), p. 71.

11. *Fairchild's Financial Manual of Retail Stores* (1978).
12. Corporate histories from *Moody's Industrial Manual* (1978).
13. *Discount Merchandiser* (January 1978), p. 105.
14. David A. Loehwing, "Discounters Discounted," *Barron's* (April 22, 1963), p. 10.
15. David A. Loehwing, "Trouble in the Store," *Barron's* (July 21, 1969), p. 3.
16. "Grant's Goes Under," *Time* (October 13, 1975), p. 64.
17. "Ten Years of Discount Retailing," *Discount Store News* (December 11, 1972), p. 3.
18. Eleanore Carruth, "K-Mart Has to Open Some New Doors on the Future," *Fortune* (July 1977), p. 150.
19. "The True Look of the Discount Industry," *Discount Merchandiser* (Annual Special Issues, 1960–1978).

Selected Sources

Tom Mahoney and Leonard Sloane, *The Great Merchants* (New York, New York: Harper & Row, 1974).

Fairchild's Financial Manual of Retail Stores (1976, 1978).

U.S. Department of Commerce, *Department Store Retailing in an Era of Change* (June 1975).

"Origins of the Chains: The Innovators," *Discount Store News* (December 11, 1972).

"Food Folk Went Discount From Scratch or Catch," *Department Store News* (December 11, 1972).

Moody's Industrial Manual (1978).

David A. Loehwing, "Trouble in the Store," *Barron's* (July 21, 1969).

Steven H. Star, "Sears, Roebuck & Company" (Boston, Massachusetts: Harvard Business School, Intercollegiate Case Clearing House, No. 4-179-123, rev. 2/79).

Chapter 3

MACROECONOMICS, DEMOGRAPHICS, AND THE FATE OF RETAIL TRADE

The remarkable transformation of the department store industry which began as early as the turn of the century came about because of the demands of competition and because of the innovative genius of notable entrepreneurs like the Filene brothers, Marty ("Grandaddy") Chase, and Lester Palestine. Ever-changing government policies have also, although sometimes unintentionally, had a major hand in shaping the corporate ownership structures that are identified with the industry today. While recognizing the significance of competitive forces, human ingenuity, and government policy, it is essential not to underrate the tremendous impact of broad demographic and macro-economic trends upon the development of the industry. The past, present, and future of a given firm and of the industry as a whole is inextricably linked to the aggregate social and economic trends of the region, nation, or global community in which it operates.

Retail trade and service industries differ from manufacturing in that the demand for their goods is primarily derived from income generated in other sectors. Population growth, variations in disposable income, inflation and recession, technological advances in transportation and communication, and changes in consumer credit practices all affect where and how much is spent by consumers. The health of the industry is consequently subject to these forces and to particular stages in the industrial and cultural development of a region. Retail trade cannot lead the economic development of a region; its direct reliance upon consumer demand dictates that it must necessarily follow.

Focusing on demographic, economic, and technological trends will help to clarify the relationship of these factors to the dramatic historical transformation of the department store industry.

Population

During the 1950's, the average annual rate of population growth in New England, the Mid-Atlantic, West North-Central, and East South-Central states lagged behind the nationwide average of 1.7 percent (see Table 3.1). During this same period the regions exhibiting greater than average rates of growth were the Pacific, Mountain, South Atlantic, and East North-Central states (see Figure 3.1).

During the 1960's and 1970's, while the population growth of the United States as a whole began to slow as a result of declining birth rates, a continuation of the regional growth trends of the 1950's could be seen in every region except the East North-Central.

Manufacturing, once a mainstay of the New England economy, declined steadily in the region, preferring locations in the South and abroad which offered cheaper labor, land, energy, and taxes. Since 1966 manufacturing employment has declined by more than 10 percent in the Northeast overall but has increased in the rest of the United States by a more than equal amount. Reduced employment opportunities in the North and a new image of the South as a place to enjoy "the good life" have encouraged this exodus.

The Mid-Atlantic region has exhibited a population growth pattern similar to that seen in New England since 1960. Manufacturing has been declining rapidly, ceding to service-sector employment, particularly in the past ten years. The steeper decline seen in the Mid-Atlantic states than in the nation as a whole can be attributed to the escape of New York City residents to outlying suburban areas in New England and the cumulative effects of the Sunbelt migration.

In the East North-Central states—Wisconsin, Michigan, Illinois, Indiana, and Ohio—the population decline has been steeper than in any other region during the 25-year-period between 1950 and 1975. The combined forces of Sunbelt migration and the decline of farming help to explain this phenomenon. The region benefited from a higher growth rate during the 1950's than the nation as a whole because of the boom in the auto industry and related manufacturing industries such as rubber and steel. Increased reliance upon the automobile resulting from the growth of the American suburbs spurred the increased production of automobiles during this decade. Production

Table 3.1. Population by Region, 1950–1975 (thousands)

	1950	1960	1970	1975	1950–1960	1960–1970	1970–1975
New England	9,314	10,532	11,883	12,198	1.2%	1.2%	.6%
Mid-Atlantic	30,164	34,468	37,199	37,263	1.3	.9	.3
E. No.-Central	30,399	36,226	40,252	40,979	1.8	1.1	.4
W. No.-Central	14,061	15,394	16,319	16,690	.9	.6	.5
So. Atlantic	21,182	25,972	30,671	33,715	2.1	1.7	1.9
E. So.-Central	11,477	12,050	12,803	13,544	.5	.6	1.1
W. So.-Central	14,538	16,951	19,321	20,855	1.5	1.3	1.5
Mountain	5,075	6,855	8,282	9,644	3.1	1.9	3.1
Pacific	15,115	21,198	26,523	28,234	3.4	2.3	1.3
United States	151,326	179,975	203,810	213,121	1.7	1.3	.9

SOURCE: U.S. Bureau of the Census, *Current Population Reports*, Series P–25.

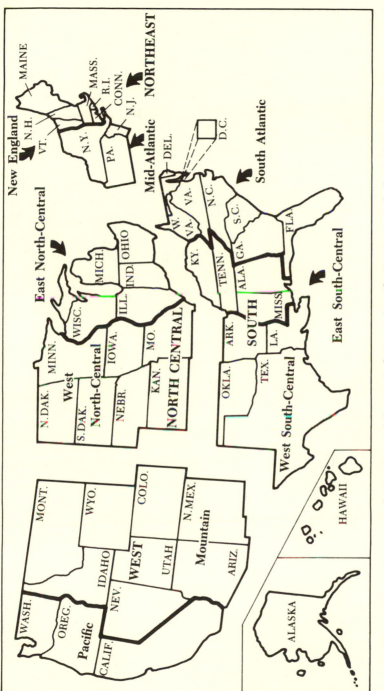

Figure 3.1. Regions and Divisions of the United States (Pacific Division including Alaska and Hawaii).

required new workers, many of whom were recruited from the South.

In the ensuing period, however, auto, tire, and steel production were continually exported to other parts of the country. As a result, employment opportunity declined in the industrial heartland. With it came a decline in population growth as out-migration increased.

The West North-Central states suffered an even worse bout of out-migration as a consequence of the decline in family farming. The migration pattern was so pronounced that net population growth throughout the region was among the lowest in the nation. In the generation between 1950 and 1975 the West South-Central region expanded by only 2.5 million people, while the United States as a whole grew by over 60 million.

In sharp contrast, the South Atlantic and West South-Central regions grew dramatically over the same period. Almost 19 million more people lived in these twelve states in 1975 compared with the number in 1950. The growth of Southern manufacturing and extraction—particularly in chemicals, steel, and oil—highlighted this growth. Millions moved to take advantage of employment there, while millions of elderly moved to Florida and other parts of the South to enjoy their retirement. With new communities springing up throughout the region, retail and service establishments flourished. The New South became a land of opportunity for the entrepreneur (see Figure 3.2).

The Deep South—Alabama, Mississippi, Tennessee, and Kentucky—fared considerably worse. The mass exodus of blacks from the Mississippi delta and other agricultural areas made this part of the South the slowest-growth region in the country in both the 1950's and the 1960's. It was not until the end of the black farm worker exodus that these states grew at a faster pace than the nation as a whole. The great Sunbelt migration came late to this area.

The Mountain and Pacific regions have grown more rapidly than the nation as a whole during all three decades. The phenomenal growth of these two regions plus the South Atlantic was greater than in all other regions combined. Again, the relocation and expansion of manufacturing industries has been responsible for such high rates of growth.

One must note, however, that growth within regions is as highly uneven as between them. For example, in New England in the 1950's, the population of Connecticut grew almost twice as fast as the region as a whole, partly as a result of the mass migration from New York City. Its growth continued in the 1960's but, for all practical

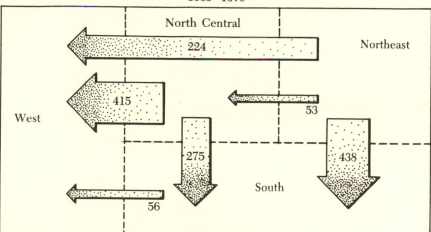

1965–1970

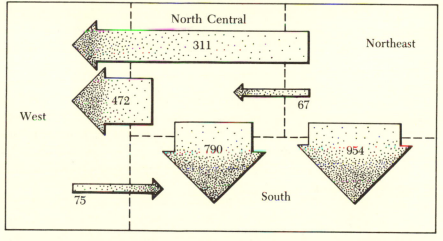

1970–1975

Figure 3.2. Net Interregional Migration, 1965–1970 and 1970–1975. The width of the arrows is proportional to the volume of net interregional migration flows. The figures accompanying the arrows indicate numbers of net migrants in thousands. (*Sources: Bureau of the Census, U.S. Department of Commerce, Census of Population: 1970. Bureau of the Census, U.S. Department of Commerce, Mobility of the Population of the United States. March 1970–March 1975, Series P-20, No. 285* in Current Population Reports. *Reprinted from Brian J. L. Berry and Donald C. Dahmann, "Population Distribution in the United States in the 1970s," Assembly of Behavioral and Social Sciences, National Research Council, National Academy of Sciences, 1977.*)

purposes, came to a halt in the early 1970's. The region's northern tier of states (Maine, New Hampshire, and Vermont) is now the fastest growing section in New England as manufacturing industry has moved away from the Boston-New York-Washington corridor in search of lower wages, lower taxes, and weaker unions. This is especially true for New Hampshire, where "runaway" plants from Massachusetts have settled across the border creating boom-town conditions in communities such as Manchester and Nashua. The 2 percent annual growth rate experienced by the Granite State during the early 1970's is more than double the U.S. rate and higher than any other region with the exception of the Mountain states. In contrast, tiny Rhode Island experienced an actual decline in population, and Connecticut and Massachusetts grew by less than half a percent per year.

Primarily as a result of the growth in the northern tier, New England as a whole has experienced faster population growth since the 1960's than the Mid-Atlantic states and the North-Central region. However, as described above, the rest of the nation has grown faster, with the Sunbelt and Mountain states being the primary recipients of "Frostbelt" out-migration. Each of these trends is summarized in Figure 3.2.

The relative slowdown in national population growth is reflected in forecasts to the year 1990, when the population growth rate is expected by the Commerce Department to pick up sharply. Census projections for New England suggest that the population will grow to 14.5 million by the end of the century from 12.2 million in 1975. This is a continuation of the current .6 percent annual growth rate, which compares with a projected .8 percent increase for the country as a whole (see Figure 3.3). The Mountain states and the South Atlantic region are projected to continue to lead the nation in population growth, while the Mid-Atlantic and East North-Central states (New York, New Jersey, and Pennsylvania) will hardly grow at all. The difference between regions can be attributed to predicted differences in migration rates and variations in regional age profiles.

These population trends alone provide an explanation for the tremendous regional variation in department store sales and capital expansion discussed later in this chapter. The direct reliance of the industry upon consumer spending suggests that rapid population growth in an area, caused by relocation or expansion decisions in other economic sectors such as manufacturing, will generate a larger volume of retail sales. Such increases represent an opportunity for

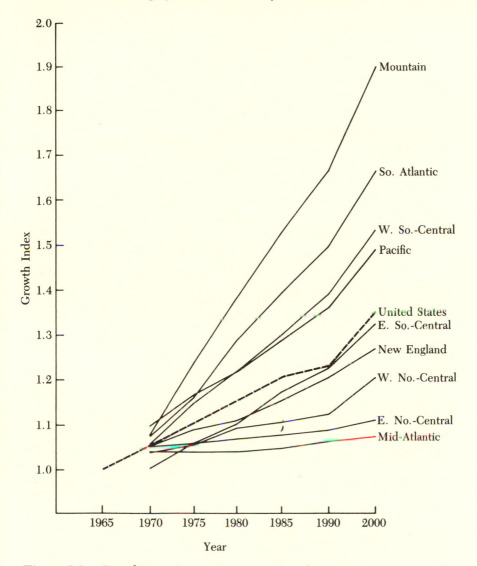

Figure 3.3.   Population Forecasts to Year 2000 by Region (1965 = 1.00). (*Source: Bureau of the Census, U.S. Department of Commerce, Series P-25, No. 735, October 1978.*)

existing retail firms to capture a greater market share through expansion. They also open the door for the entry of new firms into the market. Of course, how powerful an incentive exists for expansion or new entry depends on the affluence of the population. Per capita income is a good measure of this factor.

Per Capita Income

Consumer spending varies between regions in rough proportion to disposable income. Per capita incomes in New England, the Mid-Atlantic, Pacific, and East North-Central states have grown less quickly than per capita incomes in the nation as a whole, with the result that as a group they have approached the national average over the eighteen-year period shown in Figure 3.4. Conversely, per capita income growth in the South Atlantic, West North-Central, and Mountain states has outstripped that of the Northeast and Pacific, reaching near-parity with the national average by 1978. Even the East South-Central states, which still lag considerably behind national levels of per capital income, have shown dramatic increases in earnings, growing by 54 percent between 1967 and 1972 and by 64 percent in the 1972–1977 period (see Table 3.2). Thus over the past two decades a distinct trend toward equalization of per capita income

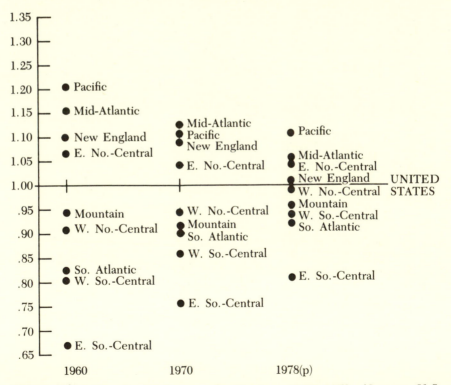

Figure 3.4. Per Capita Income by Region, 1960–1978. (*Source: U.S. Bureau of Economic Analysis, Survey of Current Business, August 1974, April 1975, and April 1979.*)

Table 3.2.   Per Capita Income (Current Dollars) by Region, 1963–1977

	1963	1967	1972	1977	Percentage Change in Per Capita Income		
					1963–1967	*1967–1972*	*1972–1977*
New England	2,766	3,495	4,754	7,183	26.4	36.0	51.1
Mid-Atlantic	2,810	3,590	5,005	7,460	27.8	39.4	49.1
E. No.-Central	2,608	3,389	4,699	7,347	30.0	38.7	56.4
W. No.-Central	2,332	3,012	4,281	6,830	29.2	42.1	59.5
So. Atlantic	2,083	2,749	4,131	6,536	32.0	50.3	58.2
E. So.-Central	1,664	2,241	3,448	5,651	34.7	53.9	63.9
W. So.-Central	1,961	2,606	3,849	6,458	32.9	47.7	67.8
Mountain	2,292	2,818	4,158	6,589	22.9	47.6	58.5
Pacific	2,871	3,597	4,880	7,820	25.3	35.7	60.2
United States	2,449	3,159	4,478	7,019	29.0	41.8	56.7

SOURCE: U.S. Bureau of Economic Analysis, *Survey of Current Business*, August 1974, April 1975, and August 1979.

among regions has emerged, as shown in Figure 3.4. This phenomenon, largely the product of growing industrialization in the Sunbelt, has had a pronounced effect on spatial patterns of growth in the department store industry.

As with population, differences in income within a region are as striking as those between regions. For example, in New England in 1973, Connecticut had the highest per capita income in the country, while Maine was ranked 43rd among the states, Massachusetts was 12th, Rhode Island 24th, New Hampshire 30th, and Vermont 39th. The combination of population decline and low per capita income, other things equal, would suggest that Rhode Island will not be a prime location for further department store development. The same may be true for Maine and (perhaps) Vermont despite their population growth. In contrast, New Hampshire's retail sector should benefit from the favorable trend in both population and income.

Equalization of income between regions, one would think, would be reflected in consumption and therefore in retail sales. Such is clearly the case as shown in Table 3.3. The rapid expansion in department store sales in the West South-Central, Mountain, and Pacific regions reflect the above-average growth in both population and income, while the recent declines in real sales volume in New England and the Mid-Atlantic states come in response to relatively smaller increases on each score. The health of the industry in each region is thus closely linked to demographic and economic trends. In fact, when statistical analysis is applied to the data, it is found that

Table 3.3.   Percentage Change in Real Department Store Sales (1967 Dollars) by
              Region, 1963–1977

	1963–1967	1967–1972	1972–1977
New England	50.8	29.5	−5.1
Mid. Atlantic	44.7	23.8	−6.6
E. No.-Central	50.7	26.1	5.7
W. No.-Central	42.4	31.9	14.4
So. Atlantic	57.4	50.1	10.7
E. So.-Central	54.9	63.6	14.4
W. So.-Central	62.5	29.9	29.4
Mountain	45.9	59.9	23.8
Pacific	43.1	27.1	17.6
United States	49.3	32.3	8.9

SOURCE: U.S. Bureau of the Census, *Census of Retail Trade*, 1963, 1967, 1972, 1977.

over three-quarters of the variance in regional department store sales can be explained by differences in aggregate regional personal income. It is precisely in this sense that the retail sector cannot lead economic development, but must necessarily follow it. The remaining 25 percent of the variance could presumably be explained by interregional differences in the modes of retail trade as well as differences in such factors as consumer preference, the age of the population, and the availability of consumer credit.

Consumer Credit

Indeed, the expansion of the retail sector during the 1950's was fueled by an explosion in credit. In 1950 the ratio of credit to disposable income was 10.4 percent, with $21.5 billion worth of debt outstanding. Only a decade later, the ratio to disposable income had grown to 16.1 percent and the total debt outstanding stood at $56.1 billion. By 1976 the sheer amount of credit had grown by another fourfold to $217.8 billion, but the ratio had leveled off at 18.4 percent after peaking at almost 20 percent in 1973 (see Table 3.4). The leveling off in consumer debt at under one-fifth of disposable income, tied to a growth in delinquency, indicates that unless dramatic changes occur in consumer credit policies, there will be no new explosion in debt similar to that in the 1950's. Indeed, the engineered credit crunch in early 1980, which was hardly viewed as helpful by department store executives, reinforces this conclusion.

Table 3.4.   Consumer Credit, 1950–1977

	1950	1960	1970	1973	1976
Credit Outstanding (billions of dollars)	$21.5	$56.1	$127.0	$179.0	$217.8
Ratio to Disposable Income	10.4%	16.1%	18.5%	19.8%	18.4%
Delinquency Rate (30 days & over, percentage of installment debt)	2.20%	1.93%	2.14%	2.53%	2.57%

SOURCE: American Bankers Association (Washington, D.C.)

Technological Change and Other Factors

Changes in packaging, warehousing, transportation, and inventory control have also helped to reshape the industry, boosting sales per worker and increasing the number of variety of goods available. Changes in communications have influenced advertising practices and have enabled large-scale department and discount concerns to take advantage of scale economies in media promotional efforts.

In addition to the above factors, which affect the form or size of the industry at a national or regional level, there are localized phenomena which affect the viability of the industry at the community level. For example, lifestyle and buying practices vary greatly within regions. Also of importance is the economic base of the community within which a department store is located. If a large percentage of local employment is engaged by one industry, then the fate of local department stores is linked to the fate of that industry. A community with a broad economic base encompassing a variety of industries will be less vulnerable to fluctuations in any particular sector of the economy. For example, one would expect that department stores in the Seattle, Washington, area, so dependent on aircraft production, or in Groton, Connecticut, with its massive General Dynamics shipyard relying on submarine contracts, would be especially hard hit by fluctuations in defense spending.

Still, the actual growth in trade, especially the relative growth *between individual retail modes,* is not uniquely determined by any of these factors. The changing ownership structure of the industry and increased market concentration affect the level of expansion in a number of ways.

Market Concentration in the
Department Store Industry

A look at the sales figures of independent retailers and multi-unit firms is helpful in illustrating the degree of ownership concentration which exists overall in the industry. Although ownership structures reflect a wider variety of forms than examined here, the figures indicate a rapid trend toward increasing concentration and signal the demise of the independently owned firm. The numbers themselves paint a portrait eerily reminiscent of the merger movement days in manufacturing nearly two generations ago.

In 1972 there were two million retail firms in the United States, ranging from small boutiques to department store chains owning thousands of outlets.[1] Only 290,000 of these had multi-unit establishments, but these were responsible for over $300 billion of the $449 billion in total sales. Only 74,000 (less than 4 percent) had sales in excess of one million dollars, while 56 percent of all multi-unit sales went through firms owning more than 100 units each. Between 1948 and 1972, the percent of total sales made through multi-unit firms rose from 29.6 percent to 44.0 percent.[2]

Among department stores, multi-unit structure and economic concentration is much more pervasive than in the retail sector as a whole, and it is growing over time as single-unit independents disappear or are acquired by holding companies. In 1970, 85.5 percent of all department stores sales were attributed to multi-unit firms (operating eleven or more retail stores). Only six years later, 90 percent of sales went through chain stores or holding companies.[3] Capital expenditures were even more concentrated among the chains, accounting for 89 percent of all department store investment in 1972.

Within the general merchandise category, which includes variety stores and a range of old fashioned general stores made famous in New England and the "wild west," department stores are responsible for more than 80 percent of all sales. An examination of data on the leading general merchandise chains reveals that concentration is growing rapidly even *within* the group of largest merchandisers. In 1967 the top 32 firms in the industry accounted for three-quarters of total sales; by 1977 this group accounted for seven-eighths (see Table 3.5). Moreover, within the sales of the top 32, the largest five increased their market share from 49.8 percent in 1967 to over 60 percent a decade later. This represents market concentration equal to that in many manufacturing industries. These five alone (Sears, K-Mart, J.C. Penney, Woolworth's, and Federated) accounted for *one-*

Table 3.5.   Concentration in the General Merchandise Industry Sales, 1967, 1977

	1967	1977
Billions of Dollars		
General Merchandise Sales-Total	41.0	89.2
Top 32	31.0	77.8
Top 5	10.8	47.0
Percentage		
General Merchandise Sales-Total	100.0%	100.0%
Top 32/Total	75.6	87.2
Top 5/Top 32	49.8	60.4
Top 5/Total	26.3	52.7

SOURCE: U.S. Bureau of Census, *Census of Retail Trade and Fairchild's Financial Manual of Retail Sales, 1967–1978.*

half of all general merchandise sales in the nation in 1977—double their share in 1967.

Increasing sales concentration ratios reveal, perhaps more than any other statistic, the growth in the relative importance of the large holding company and department store chain. This conclusion is further reinforced by examining sales data for individual firms. Sales volume for the top 32 companies increased four times over between 1963 and 1977. The top five retailers had growth factors ranging from a low of 3.4 (Sears) to a phenomenal 18.3 for K-Mart (see Table 3.6).

It is possible to make only a crude estimate of the growth in each mode of retail production within the industry. The estimate is not precise because we have data for only the 32 largest companies, and because individual firms increasingly control operations in more than one mode (for example, Federated is both a holding company of full-service department stores and an operator of a number of discount department store chains). Nevertheless, the sales data suggest

Table 3.6.   Growth Index for Leading Retailers (1963 = 1.00), 1963–1977

Top 32	3.99
Top 5	4.37
Sears	3.37
K-Mart	18.29
J.C. Penney	5.11
F.W. Woolworth	4.68
Federated	4.36

SOURCE: Calculated from data in *Fairchild's Financial Manual of Retail Sales, 1963–1977.*

Table 3.7.   Growth Among Department Store Modes (1963 = 1.00) 1963–1977

	Sales		Growth Factor
	1963	1977	
Department Store Chains	11,973,820	39,600,000*	3.30
Holding Companies	4,006,085	18,952,543	4.73
Discount Department Stores	3,521,960	19,213,088	5.45

SOURCE: Calculated from data in *Fairchild's Financial Manual of Retail Sales, 1963–1977.*

* Estimate required for no separate reporting of Montgomery-Ward after acquisition by Mobil Oil Co.

that discount chains are growing most rapidly, followed by holding companies and department store chains (see Table 3.7).

Given the lower payroll/sales ratio in the discount mode, this naturally does not bode well for employment in the industry. Decreased reliance upon labor is a by-product of concentrated ownership. Through the medium of advanced technology and advertising, which are only cost-effective when applied on a large scale, giant firms seek to reduce their payrolls wherever possible. The dominance of the discount mode and the growing proportion of market share accounted for by discount department store sales suggests that in the future the need for employees in the industry as a whole will increase much less quickly than in times past.

Regional Growth and Decline

Unfortunately there are no analogous sales data by region, and consequently it is not possible to directly document regional changes in industry concentration or relative growth by mode of operation. The alternative is to consult Dun & Bradstreet data on the number of establishments by ownership mode in, for example, the New England region. Tabulations on the Dun & Bradstreet data suggest that in New England, as in the nation overall, there has been a shift toward department store chains and holding companies relative to independents. This shift is shown in Table 3.8. Each of the Dun & Bradstreet sample periods is independent; thus comparisons of raw data across years are not reliable. Within each period, however, the samples are generally random so that disaggregation by ownership type should reflect the underlying establishment population.

As a proportion of total establishments, independent department stores have declined from a quarter of all outlets to less than a sixth in

Table 3.8.   Dun & Bradstreet Random Sample of Department Stores in New England by Mode of Ownership, 1969, 1972, 1974

	1969		1972		1974	
	No.	*%*	*No.*	*%*	*No.*	*%*
Independent	106	25.7	102	20.0	97	16.2
Headquarters/Branch	268	65.0	348	68.1	422	70.5
Parent/Subsidiary	38	9.2	61	11.9	80	13.4
	412	100.0	511	100.0	599	100.0

SOURCE: Special tabulations on Dun & Bradstreet Establishment data prepared by David Birch, Laboratory for Neighborhood and Regional Change, M.I.T. (May 1979).

New England. Department store chains, including discount houses, have expanded their share of the market from 65 to 70.5 percent, while holding companies such as Federated and Allied have expanded from less than 10 percent of the market to 13.4 percent. In growth terms, this pattern is identical to the national picture, with holding companies expanding faster than department store chains and both growing relative to independents.

Trends in Department Store Profits

While the department store industry has clearly become more concentrated, existing net income (profit) figures suggest the industry is nevertheless becoming more competitive. Data on the ratio of net income to total sales shows a steady erosion in profit rates for at least the top 32 General Merchandisers taken as a group. The net income/sales ratio peaked in 1965 at 3.6 percent and fell almost steadily to 3.2 percent before plummeting to 2.2 during the 1974–1975 recession. Recovery through 1977 brought the rate up to only 3.2 percent (see Figure 3.5). The decline between 1965 and 1973 came during a period of solid sales advances and certainly cannot be exclusively attributed to a serious decline in the economy.

Ironically, the sharpest drop in reported profit rates came among the top five merchandisers. While the top 32 showed a 12.5 percent decline in the rate between 1965 and 1977, the top five reported a 14.5 percent reduction (see Figure 3.6). Leading this decline was Woolworths (−67.2%), with Federated (−24.7%) following a rather distant second. Over the period, however, average net profit rates among the top five were still 23 percent higher than among the top 32 (3.90 vs. 3.16 percent).

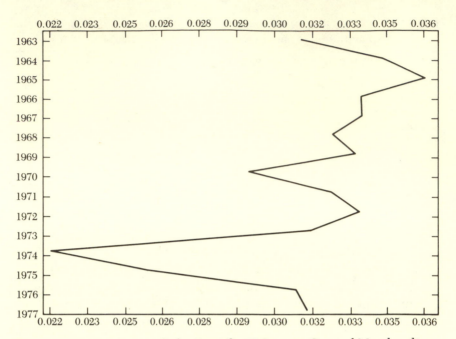

Figure 3.5.   Net Income/Sales Ratio for 32 Largest General Merchandisers, 1963–1977. (*Source: Fairchild's Financial Manual of Retail Trade, 1963–1977*.)

While there are no comparable published data on net income/sales ratios for independents, the large number of bankruptcies plus information obtained through interviews with executives of existing independents suggest that profits are indeed lower in this sector. Most sources suggest that a 2 percent ratio is not uncommon. The independent stores that survive appear to do so despite low profits primarily because family members have more than an economic stake in the enterprise.

On a share equity (profit on assets) basis, net income for the top 32 merchandisers ranged between 8.6 percent and 12.9 percent annually, with an average of 11.3 percent over the entire period. While the variance among firms was substantial, the net income for the top five firms was slightly higher than for the top 32, with a 12.5 percent average. The average 1963–1977 net income/share equity ratios for seven of the leading department store holding companies and chains are shown in Table 3.9. The figures range from a low of 5.9 percent for Montgomery Ward to a high of 14.8 percent for J.C. Penney.

Despite these healthy profit margins on assets, low margins on sales make this industry susceptible to violent turn-arounds in the

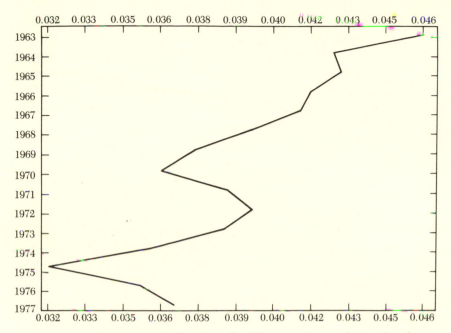

Figure 3.6. Net Income/Sales Ratio for 5 Largest General Merchandisers, 1963–1977. (*Source: Fairchild's Financial Manual of Retail Trade, 1963–1978.*)

economic well-being of individual firms. The inability to contain costs even in light of booming sales can turn a 3–4 percent net income/sales ratio into a substantial loss.

Two cases clearly illustrate this point. In the period between 1963 and 1969, Arlan's Discount Department stores recorded a sales boom of more than 160 percent, from $139 million in business to $364 million in seven years. This compares with a 91 percent growth for the top 32 firms. During this entire period, the number of Arlan's outlets grew from 40 to 111.[4] A year later there were 119. An average

Table 3.9. **Average Net Income/Share Equity Ratios for Leading Department Store Firms, 1963–1977**

J.C. Penney	14.8
Federated	13.6
K-Mart	13.5
Sears	13.0
F.W. Woolworth	9.1
Allied	9.0
Montgomery–Ward	5.9

SOURCE: *Fairchild's Financial Manual of Retail Trade, 1963–1977.*

net income/share equity return of an extraordinary 19.4 percent during the halcyon years provided much of the capital needed for this expansion. Nonetheless, two years later Arlan's was forced to file for bankruptcy as their sales margin (net income/sales ratio) fell further and further below 2 percent and finally turned negative in 1970.[5] Industry sources attribute Arlan's demise to an almost fanatical desire to expand at any cost, poor management, inadequately researched location decisions, and insufficient attention to their cost structure.

The failure of W.T. Grant can be traced to similar factors. In the years before it was forced to close its doors, sales exceeded $1.8 billion. Between 1963 and 1972, its net income/share equity ratio averaged 13 percent, somewhat better than the industry as a whole. Following its attempt to enter the hard goods market with a massive inventory investment outlay, its profit rate plunged to 3.7 percent in 1973, followed by a huge loss in 1974.[6] Unable to pay its creditors in light of the 1974 loss, Grant's was forced into bankruptcy the following year. It was one of the great business crashes of all time, affecting more than 75,000 employees and 1,100 stores.[7]

Retail Saturation and Regional Markets

Today throughout the industry there is widespread concern about the possible "saturation" of the retail market, particularly in the New England and Mid-Atlantic regions. Generally, a community or region is considered saturated at the point that retail growth becomes a zero-sum game; that is, when each retail establishment can expand its sales only at the expense of one or more other stores. Disregarding population and income growth, it is reasonable to expect that there is a maximum level attainable by department store sales in a particular region and that, once that level has been reached, retail businesses can grow only at the expense of their competitors.

Although New England was the site of rapid retail growth during the 1960's, particularly in discounting, department store executives there suggest that the industry faced market saturation by the late 1970's. In the words of one industry source:

> I would guess the retail industry today is closer to being a zero-sum game than a growing industry. There is a market here and it is available to those who go after it and essentially take it away from somebody else. . . . Retail is a take-away proposition and will remain so until New England finds a way to have built-in thrust for its economic activity. . . . It is a static market and our strategy is just that—

aggressive search for areas with purchasing power and a constant effort to make our business look attractive.

In New England's zero-sum game, aggressive firms appear to be able to capture market share from their competitors only if they are exceptionally innovative in their merchandising concepts and location strategies.

Some of the problems experienced by retail firms in an increasingly saturated market are illustrated by the comments of one executive:[8]

When Federated (Department Stores) first started to aggressively build branch stores in the early 60's, the branches were sure successes. They were built in those areas with the highest population density and the highest income level. It was a case of bringing our downtown headquarters concept to the suburbs.

Now we've move beyond the first ring of branches to the second ring, and sometimes to the third ring. What happens is obvious. There isn't the population and income to support full-line stores in many of these outlying regions. Although there are still opportunities in the better areas, sometimes the effect is to transfer substantial volume from our existing stores.[8]

Increased levels of saturation can result not only in increased competition between firms but also in increased competition *within* firms—for example, between chain outlets owned by the same firm or between branches held by the same parent company. Under such circumstances, a firm which continues to grow must build smaller stores, change advertising methods, or carefully plan new store locations in an effort to minimize the effects of saturation. Without altering its retail strategies accordingly, an expansion program may be detrimental rather than beneficial to a firm's well-being.

The measure of saturation generally accepted by the retail industry is the ratio of the number of households to the number of stores in any given area. Figure 3.7 depicts the change in this ratio for discount department stores in New England and in the United States as a whole during the 10-year period from 1967 to 1977. Again, as an example of the differences which exist not only between regions but also within them, Figure 3.8 shows the same statistics for each of the six New England states.

It is clear that New England has more stores per household than the rest of the country, although the United States as a whole began to catch up with New England after 1972. From this year on, growth in the number of stores in New England lagged behind household growth, suggesting that saturation had taken place. The ratio con-

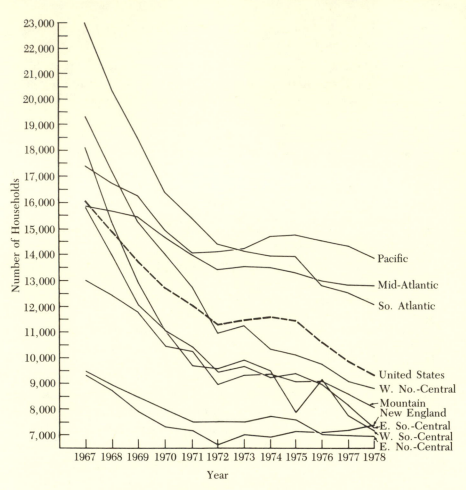

Figure 3.7. Number of Households per Discount Store in the United States and Regions. (*Source: "True Look of the Discount Industry,"* Discount Merchandiser, *June 1967–1978.*)

tinues to decline in the United States, however, implying that other regions have not yet reached the point of a zero-sum game.

One should not presume, however, that saturation is static. For example, Massachusetts, which had as many stores in 1977 as it had in 1972, was "less saturated" in 1977 because population growth of the preceding five years had not been offset by new store construction. On the other hand, if an area were to experience a wave of out-migration or a decrease in per capita income, saturation might increase even in the absence of new store construction.

Which regions are still experiencing growth and which have

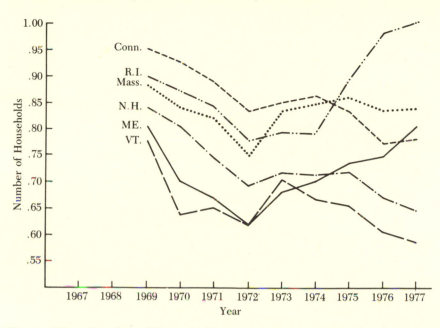

Figure 3.8. Number of Households per Discount Store in the New England States (1967 = 1.00). (*Source: "True Look of the Discount Industry,"* Discount Merchandiser, *June 1967–1978.*)

leveled off can be seen in Figures 3.7 and 3.9. The regions of the Northeast and the industrial Midwest, as well as the Pacific coast, all seem to have reached "saturation ratio" plateaus after 1970. This is particularly clear in Figure 3.9, where the household/store ratio is indexed to its 1967 value in each region. Population density, store size, the dispersion of outlets, the level of disposable income, and the market share captured by each retail mode, account for differences in the absolute *level* of the ratio between regions. Thus areas with very different ratios can still be equally saturated. The Pacific region with nearly 14,000 households per store is found to be nearly as saturated as New England with only 7,500.

The Southern regions and the Mountain states all continue to experience rapid expansion in the number of retail outlets relative to the number of households, despite their much faster-growing populations. This clearly reflects the Sunbelt boom in department store construction and indirectly provides evidence of the capital shift to the South. The migration of the manufacturing base, once centered in the Northeast and industrial Midwest, has obviously signaled profit opportunities for the department store industry. The firms have not hesitated to take advantage of them.

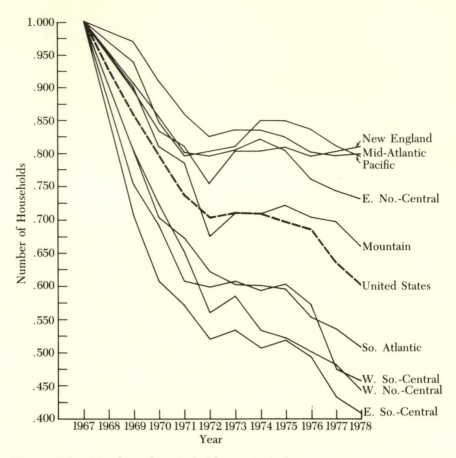

Figure 3.9. Number of Households per Store by Region, 1967–1978 (1967 = 1.00). (*Source: "True Look of the Discount Industry,"* Discount Merchandiser, *June 1967–1978.*)

Further evidence of the regional tendency toward saturation is provided for the New England region by Dun & Bradstreet data presented in Table 3.10. Between 1969 and 1972 the total number of births (+ in-migrations) of establishments exceeded department store deaths (+ out-migrations) by more than 2.6 to 1 in the New England region. But by the period 1974–1976 (admittedly during a recession), the number of deaths far exceeded the number of newly established units. Although Dun & Bradstreet samples in each period are not strictly comparable because of changes in the sampling ratio over time, the trends are strong enough to confirm this regional tendency toward saturation.

Market saturation, of course, has serious implications for the future

Table 3.10. **Gross Change in Number of Department Store Establishments in New England, 1969–1976**

	Total in Initial Year	Net Change	Births & In-Migrations	Deaths & Out-Migrations	Ratio
1969–1972	297	+92	+150	− 58	2.6:1
1972–1974	457	+67	+128	− 61	2.1:1
1974–1976	545	−76	+100	−176	.6:1

SOURCE: Dun & Bradstreet Data prepared by David Birch, Laboratory for Neighborhood and Regional Change, M.I.T. (May 1979).

of the industry in New England as well as in other regions. Although the population of New England is expected to increase between now and the year 2000 (recall Figure 3.3), neither population nor disposable income is expected to expand sufficiently to allow a return to the rapid department store expansion of the 1950's and 1960's. Moreover, in the states with unused physical capacity where the number of department stores has fallen in recent years, there may be future expansion of sales without an equivalent expansion in new-store construction.

All of this notwithstanding, industry sources suggest that there will still be room for a store which has a "better concept" even in a saturated market. Some small independents may survive if they are able to appeal to consumers on some basis other than price. A firm able to tap a new market or win over a particular group of customers may prosper even under adverse conditions. Some firms continue to pursue increased market share in saturated regions. K-Mart, the retail giant, has no hesitation about expanding into New England or other regions which already have well-developed discount chains and high levels of retail saturation. "New England's not saturated with K-Mart's" seems to be the prevailing attitude. Although K-Mart is a newcomer in New England, it has the financial strength to quickly grow in the market at the expense of other firms.

As one might imagine, increasing retail saturation is affecting the whole character of the industry. Strong firms capable of growth in a saturated market are able to take advantage of economies of scale when they expand, and thereby obtain the means for continued growth. Saturation does not eliminate the incentive to expand, but it does dictate that there will be "losers" as well as "winners" in the competitive arena. The disadvantages of smallness and high costs appear to have made independents the direct casualties of chain store expansion. Another casualty may be employment. With the rapid growth in the number of outlets before saturation was achieved, employment levels in the older regions of the country grew accordingly. Now with the number of stores remaining roughly constant in these regions, the employment boom is over. Indeed, as competition stiffens, firms may move to further decrease their dependency on labor. The outlook for employment growth in the department store industry is gloomy—*how* gloomy is the subject of Chapter 5. Before we pursue this subject, however, we shall take a closer look at ownership and control in the industry, for this is where the retail revolution really begins.

Endnotes

1. U.S. Bureau of the Census, *Census of Retail Trade*, 1963, 1967, 1972, 1977.
2. U.S. Bureau of the Census, *U.S. Census of Business*, (Vols. I, IV, VI), 1948, 1972.
3. Calculated from data in *Fairchild's Financial Manual of Retail Stores*, 1967–1978.
4. "True Look of the Discount Industry," *Discount Merchandiser* (May 1964–1970).
5. *Fairchild's Financial Manual of Retail Stores*, 1967–1978.
6. *Ibid.*
7. U.S. Department of Commerce, *U.S. Industrial Outlook 1977* (January 1977), p. 208.
8. "Federated Department Stores" (Boston: Harvard Business School, Intercollegiate Case Clearing House, No. 375-147, 1976), p. 12.

Selected Sources

Fairchild's Financial Manual of Retail Trade, 1963–1978.
U.S. Bureau of the Census, *Census of Retail Trade*, 1963, 1967, 1972, 1977.
U.S. Bureau of the Census, *Estimates and Projections of the Populations of States: 1970 to 2000*, Table 1.
U.S. Bureau of the Census, *Number, Median Income, and Standard Errors in 1975 and 1969 of Families and Unrelated Individuals based on the Survey of Income and Education (SIE) and the 1970 Census for Regions, Divisions, and States*, Table 13A.

Chapter 4

OWNERSHIP, CAPITAL INVESTMENT, AND EXPANSION IN THE DEPARTMENT STORE INDUSTRY

Once the poor stepsister of America's corporate giants, department store firms now rank with the largest of the Fortune 500. Increased consumerism brought about by an expanding economy and changes in government policy toward the retail sector have promoted the growth of enormous multi-unit enterprises. The almost complete displacement of the industry's earlier *petite bourgeoisie* form by its present corporate structure has brought with it new profit criteria for investment, a diversification of the industry's capital base, and a spatial redistribution of investment. Investment decisions are now made with the national or world market as the relevant arena. Few industries have undergone such a radical transformation in such a brief period of time.

Two Forms of Ownership: Private and Corporate

Two distinct forms of ownership exist within the industry reflecting different philosophies and producing different strategies at the firm level. Privately held (or "independent") department stores are generally small, single-outlet, locally based concerns, financially responsible to a single individual or family. Corporate-held concerns, on the other hand, are almost always large, multi-store operations with

61

financial obligations well beyond the community in which their stores are located. These firms vary greatly in their internal structures, their philosophies, and their objectives, but they share a common set of operating constraints imposed by the marketplace in the form of necessary rates of return. Because of their size, they benefit from significant economies of scale which separate them from independently held businesses and contribute to their market dominance.

There is a strong correlation between the size of a company (as measured by the number of units) and its form of ownership. The only privately owned department stores encountered with any frequency are single-unit independents. No privately owned chain stores (11 or more units) or corporate-owned department stores which have less than 11 outlets were encountered in the course of our study. The ownership and size correlation explains some of the differences in acceptable levels of profitability, the availability of capital resources, and options for growth and expansion.

Privately held department stores are usually begun as family-run enterprises and tend to remain in the family until the firm goes out of business or is sold to outside interests. An example of this is Grover-Cronin, in Waltham, Massachusetts, which 93 years after its founding is still 95 percent family-owned. Like this particular firm, most independents have roots in the community in which they do business. Such roots may include family ties, or a sense of responsibility to loyal customers whose patronage has allowed the company to survive in an increasingly competitive market.

When interviewed, independent entrepreneurs stressed the vital importance of cost control, but they also mentioned that for their kind of business there are other considerations as well. "The family-held company is more apt to have someone who takes pride in running the business. . . . you can feel you are personally associated with it and your heart can get in the way of your short-run profit." Indeed, independents, because they are privately held, set their own standards for profitability to suit the priorities of the family and these standards may or may not be those which prevail for large, corporate companies.

In contrast, the centralized control of capital by corporate-held firms usually means a substantial loss of local commitment to the area in which the branch store or subsidiary is located. Corporate-held department stores sell stock and pay dividends to their shareholders. "Unlike small independents," said an executive of a former family-owned firm (now part of a large holding company), "the corporation has a commitment to its shareholders and it is far more conscious of the continuity of profit performance on a year-to-year basis. It has a commitment to constantly improving earnings." This pressure to boost profits produces the corporate-held department store's drive to grow and its drive to cut costs, often disregarding the impact of profit-enhancing measures upon the community.

Growth and cost control are a department store's main weapons in the struggle for survival. Some firms, like the rapidly expanding K-Mart chain, emphasize growth and consequently reinvest a large percentage of the company's annual earnings as expansion capital within the department store industry. Other stores, particularly established independents, concentrate on retaining rather than expanding their share of the market, and therefore focus chiefly on reducing their expenses in order to survive. Still other retail establishments follow an intermediate strategy, expanding when money is available and leveling off in times of recession.

Among corporate-held companies, a successful emphasis on growth and expanding market share is reflected in a high price/earnings ratio for the company's stock. The price/earnings ratio is generally defined as the ratio of the stock's selling price to its expected dividends. Growth stocks have high-price/earnings ratios, and investors make their money from capital gains realized when they sell their stock rather than from the dividends paid by the firm. Stores content to "hold the line" command lower ratios for their stock and must devote greater attention to the size of their dividends in order to attract investors.

Among larger companies, in particular, there is sentiment that growth is essential to survival. Not only can larger operations benefit from economies of scale and from their relative dominance in the marketplace, but some executives see growth itself as an important indicator of a company's health. When a company's growth levels off, a loss of faith in the company and in its management may ensue. "History suggests," says former head of the Council of Economic Advisors, Professor Paul McCracken, in a letter to K-Mart's chairman, "that companies which decide to 'take their ease' are apt to be on the route to decay."[1]

At the same time, the rapid growth which is taken as a sign of fiscal health can, in fact, become the cause of acute financial trouble. The head of a privately owned department store points to the difficulties which face corporate firms:

They're under pressure to open new stores to push those sales figures up and convince people that business is booming. So they take on the high cost of financing, to build or buy more locations and have to further extend their credit at these high rates to supply the new stores with fixtures, inventory, and everything else.

Each company, in its quest for growth, must find a way to grow without loading itself with debt beyond its capacity to repay its creditors. The greater a company's debt-service requirements, the greater the danger that a decline in sales, even a temporary one, will be unsustainable.

Corporate-held department stores, because of their size, have more opportunities available to them for expansion than family-owned stores. Access to scale economies generates additional capital, enabling them to expand geographically, grow internally, or diversify outside the industry. Thus, access to sufficient expansion capital is not typically an obstacle to their growth.

Private companies, on the other hand, have limited options for expansion because of their size. They are predominantly restricted to investment through "capital deepening," further investment in their existing locations. The high cost of borrowing and insufficient return on investment prevent the small firm from expanding geographically. Furthermore, the inability to multiply their outlets prevents the independent from obtaining cost savings brought about through economies of scale. Consequently, these firms generally concentrate on maintaining their local market share rather than pursuing physical expansion.

"Bigness," Economies of Scale, and the New Corporate Structure

Economies of scale can be found in nearly every facet of department store operation. Management training programs, distribution systems, buying practices, and the utilization of advertising and computer technology all provide multi-unit firms with opportunities to realize savings and increase profits that are unavailable to the independent retailer.

As a result of the increased size and corporate structure of retail firms, management training has become a major part of the department store industry. Through the use of management teams, a growing firm can distribute the costs of standardized training programs among its branch stores. The cost-effectiveness of standardizing management is illustrated by the fact that large public discount chains not only "clone" their stores but, as one industry source stated, "clone their management."[2]

The incorporation of centralized buying systems is another means by which economies of scale are achieved by larger corporate firms. The degree of centralization depends on the firm's organizational structure, but large chain stores, in particular, can take advantage of centralized buying because they are capable of placing larger-volume orders than individual branch stores. Despite the provisions of the Robinson-Patman Act (discussed further in Chapter 7), large-volume orders can be placed directly with manufacturers, thus giving retailers access to "quantity discounts" and allowing them to avoid the payment of brokerage fees which would be required of smaller private firms. Sears provides a striking example of the massive buying power of larger firms. In 1978 Sears alone accounted for 1 percent of the Gross National Product and 6 percent of all merchandise sales— excluding food, auto, and energy sales.[3] Sears' purchasing power is so vast that it has been able to purchase 65 percent of the total production of one of its suppliers, Whirlpool.[4]

As firms grow in the number of units they control, further economies of scale are to be found in the distribution network. The fixed costs of one warehouse can be spread over a greater number of stores, serving several stores almost as cheaply as it serves one or two. Companies have begun converting to centralized warehousing in the search to cut costs in as many areas as possible. Transportation costs can also be reduced if a firm locates its stores in close proximity to each other. This practice enables firms to penetrate an area thoroughly and obtain more regional market share. The success of Caldor of Norwalk, Connecticut, for example, may be partially attributed to its "clustering" of stores in three adjacent states and locating a common warehouse in Secaucus, New Jersey.

Large companies also benefit significantly from scale economies in advertising. The savings realized by distributing the fixed costs of promotional activity are directly proportional to the number of stores owned by a firm. Moreover, firms which rely most heavily on advertising to sell their products have access to even greater savings in other areas of their cost structure. Discount and conventional department store chains, for example, are now using advertising as a direct replacement for skilled labor (as discussed in greater detail in Chapter 6). Through extensive advertising campaigns, firms are able to provide enough information about their merchandise so that consumers can pre-plan their purchases, thus reducing the role of the salesperson to merely that of an order-taker or cashier.

Large chains with standardized merchandise are able to afford television spots or full-color inserts in the Sunday paper. The promotion and sales manager for one independent firm noted that his company could not come close to meeting the promotion levels which the big area chains were able to afford because of their far greater sales volume. He added that large department stores also have greater access to "co-op" advertising, where the manufacturer pays a portion of the promotion costs.

Major cost savings also result from the use of advanced technology now available to the retail industry. Again, however, access to such economy measures is available primarily to the larger firm. The substantial initial cost of the equipment can be distributed among their branch stores. Multi-unit firms use electronic data processing to more efficiently coordinate information between the central office and branch stores, decrease the size of needed inventory, and reduce a company's dependence upon skilled labor. Family-held companies are usually unable to afford such equipment, nor make cost-effective use of it.

Access to this range of scale economies produces higher profits, which can provide the retained earnings needed for further investment, if managed properly. Large corporate enterprises can thus expand even further through construction of additional outlets or by acquisition of existing stores. Uneven development within the industry is the natural outcome of these forces, with the smaller independent becoming an increasingly endangered, if not extinct, species.

Capital Sources

Whether a department store is family-held or corporate, its major source of capital is retained earnings. Management normally attempts to minimize dependency on banks and other lending institutions because borrowing involves major costs and places the firm at greater risk. The rule that internally generated funds be used for expansion holds true for nearly all stores, from the largest corporate firm to the smallest independent. K-Mart's phenomenal growth, for example, was achieved by paying out only 26 percent of its net income in the form of dividends and retaining the balance for reinvestment.[5] Federated Department Stores generally retains about half its earnings in any given year.[6]

Independent firms similarly keep their costs under control by avoiding the capital market as much as possible, seeking loans only when a cash-flow crunch dictates. Clearly the dependence on retained earnings gives a significant edge to companies with proportionately larger amounts of profit.

The manner in which companies allocate their retained earnings among various operations or branches can have a profound effect on a company's future growth. One publicly owned holding company determines the allocation of its capital resources strictly on the basis of return on investment for each retail operation. An independent, bought out by a national holding company, must compete for internal capital funds with other retail divisions across the country. Although money is available, the central office can establish a "hurdle rate," or a minimum rate of return on investment, which branches must meet in order to qualify for access to expansion funds. Furthermore, branches are not allowed to retain their own earnings at the local level. All profits must be turned over to the holding company, to be dispersed among branches which can meet or exceed the hurdle rate. Although the family-owned firm has limited investment funds, it at least maintains the freedom to determine how its limited retained earnings are to be used.

Firms desiring more rapid expansion than allowed by their level of retained earnings depend chiefly on banks and insurance companies for finance capital rather than floating additional stock. To do this requires cultivating a credible reputation with local or national lending institutions, particularly since the financial debacle of W.T. Grant and the earlier bankruptcies of firms like Interstate and Arlan's.

In 1974–1975, as inflation soared and recession hit, all but the very healthiest and most profitable stores had to cut back operations drastically. With high interest rates and low stock prices, companies modified or eliminated their expansion plans. The industry began to recover in late 1975, but it had not regained its full composure when W.T. Grant, with over a thousand stores, filed for bankruptcy on October 2. Until this giant collapsed, it was believed in the business and financial communities that the big firms were immune to the problems which beset smaller operations. Grant's bankruptcy shook the industry and all companies became conscious of the new skepticism with which financiers viewed the retail industry. As lenders realized, in the words of one executive, that "anything can go under," prospective borrowers had to work even harder to prove their soundness.

Almost universally, however, company heads agreed that problems with borrowing are problems not of availability but of cost and risk. In 1975, during the recession, the trade magazine *Discount Merchandiser* interviewed 14 heads of discount firms and found only one president who reported trouble obtaining capital. Most of the firms surveyed could borrow at the prime rate; only one company official complained that he was consistently required to pay a premium. Still, when the prime rate reaches double-digits, few firms in the industry possess investment opportunities that justify going into the capital market. The usual profit margins in the industry are too slim to permit it.

Geographic Movement of Capital

Along with changes in the investment practices and financial structure of the department store industry, there is a growing geographic movement of capital. Corporate concerns are chiefly responsible for this capital mobility because of the size of their operations and the widespread spatial distribution of their subsidiaries. Privately owned companies, for the most part, cause no relocation. Their small size confines them to a particular region and their borrowing practices are predominantly local.

Capital can be shifted geographically several times in a single investment transaction. Large firms tend to borrow from large banks, which frequently receive their funds from distant branches. This intra-bank transfer may, in itself, cause a significant capital shift. The access which many corporate firms have to a nationwide capital market may cause capital to move a second time when it is transferred from the lending institution to the department store. For example, when Zayre's 252-store regional chain based in Framingham, Massachusetts, embarked on a full-scale revitalization program, it received a $30 million loan from four major banks—Citicorp of New York, Mellon National Bank of Pittsburgh, Pennsylvania, and First Chicago and Continental Illinois banks in Chicago.[7]

When capital is invested by a firm whose operations are geographically dispersed, it may move again. For example, profits generated by a regional chain which is owned by a national holding company may be allocated to operations located in more profitable regions of the country if the regional firm is unable to meet the established hurdle rate.

This "internal capital market" is the chief means by which industry investment funds are shifted out of a region as more of the department store industry is acquired by national concerns. This is particularly likely to happen in regions such as New England, the Mid-Atlantic, East North-Central, and Pacific states, since they are relatively saturated in comparison with the rest of the nation. In this case local units of national holding companies and department store

chains are made to serve as "cash cows" for units in less developed areas of the country in which ample room for expansion still exists. As the corporate retail sector diversifies, this cash-cow status may even require outlets located in more saturated areas to indirectly bankroll distant investments in nonretail ventures.

An example of this trend is found in K-Mart. According to *Discount Store News*, K-Mart "has grown so strong financially that it can 'buy' market share from competitors by 'pricing a guy to death'." By the early 1980's it may be faced with the consequences of "the law of diminishing returns"[8] caused by market saturation in the discount sector. K-Mart's continuing operations will be throwing off far more cash than its traditional business can profitably absorb. As a result, industry sources estimate that by 1981 fully one-quarter of the company's available cash will have no place to go. One K-Mart executive told *Fortune* magazine,[9]

> The relative slowdown in the rate of discounter growth will certainly continue . . . even though discounters will do better than the market as a whole. The urgent problem now is to find some good new concepts, but this will be more difficult to find than in years past. . . . Nothing is good forever and bigness is no protection. Time is running out and we are aware of it. K-Mart must search out new directions.

The end-result of this process will be that capital made in its department store division will be transferred out of the sector. Thus K-Mart follows the pattern of other conglomerates, which frequently reinvest in regions and industries other than those in which the profits are originally made.

The corporate structure of the industry has elevated inter-store competition from the local market to the national or world level. Regional outlets of national firms must compete not only with similar stores in their own neighborhood but with their "sister" outlets across the country. This competition has forced each unit to become increasingly cost-conscious, because the competition is no longer limited to a single environment. As a result, previously inconsequential factors such as relative tax loads, transportation expenses, and utility and labor costs become very important. One executive of a New England store which is part of a national holding company is troubled by the two-percentage-point difference in local property tax costs between his store and other company units in Los Angeles, St. Louis, and Pittsburgh. Unless the store can find economies in other line items, he suggested, his unit will not be able to effectively compete for centrally controlled investment funds, and could indeed

be closed entirely. Profits may not be sufficent in the local market
to get the distant parent corporation to reinvest in the present facility.
The profit standard which each store must meet is now set nationally,
not locally.

Growth Patterns Within the Department Store
Industry: Buy-outs and Diversification

Even in saturated or near-saturated regions there are still opportunities for some expansion according to industry sources, but market
conditions require that any growth strategy be cautiously and system-
atically pursued. Uncontrolled expansion through new store construction can no longer be considered a viable formula for growth
under such circumstances. In its place the industry has generated a
series of alternative expansion strategies which take into account
increased competitive pressure. Some firms have carefully considered the suburban market while others have found a renaissance in
the central city.

Expansion into the Suburban Market

During the 1950's and 1960's, an explosion in new department store
construction followed the mass migration of city-dwellers to suburban
locations. Often the expansion spread a firm's investment base over
approximately the same number of customers as were once served by
the central city store. In order to maintain its profit margin, and
thereby continue receiving financial resources from its parent company, the firm was usually required to reduce its labor force in the
downtown stores as it created new jobs in the suburban branches.

In the 1970's, some of these same stores pursued a variant of the
suburban strategy by placing discount divisions outside the central
city. In order to maintain market share and customer loyalty, Filene's
of Boston recently expanded its automatic bargain basement concept
into the suburban market. Jordan Marsh has also built bargain basement stores and Marshall's (owned by Melville Shoe) and Hit-Or-
Miss (owned by Zayre) began suburban construction even before
Filene's received permission from its parent (Federated) to build
outside the central city. Franklin Simon, recent past President of
Filene's, assessed the situation when he observed that:[10]

> . . . . *many customers grew up using the Filene's Basement, then moved*
> *to the suburbs and shopped at Marshall's, Loehman's, and the like.*

There are X amount of dollars out there. If we don't move the business, we die.

Opening discount outlets in suburbia has lowered the sales volume of Filene's downtown basement store, but it is a necessary expansion strategy according to the company, to preserve market share in Massachusetts. Filene's believes there is an enormous market for quality merchandise at bargain prices, and therefore this new suburban gambit offers ". . . . an unlimited opportunity to get out of New England's static market."[11]

Expansion of the Central City Market

The regentrification of the central city in certain regions by middle and upper-middle income families and by individuals has provided another expansion opportunity for the retail sector. This has fostered renewed interest in cities like Providence, Rhode Island; Portland, Maine; Hartford, Connecticut; and Boston as potential markets for department stores. Boston, for example, is now experiencing a downtown renaissance with a combination of new construction and rehabilitation. The renovation of the Faneuil Hall Marketplace offers the public a new shopping facility composed of a variety of specialty stores. Before it was built, Boston banks were pessimistic about the potential success of the renovation project. As one banker reflected:[12]

I looked around and there weren't any department stores, no parking lot, no real housing. There were none of the ingredients that were key to any business, any regional center.

The venture, however, was ultimately financed by a group of New York banks with the stipulation that Boston banks carry half the total liability. Construction was cautiously pursued in three stages with final restoration costs totalling more than $30 million.[13]

Near Faneuil Hall are located Boston's two leading department stores, Jordan Marsh and Filene's, occupying first and second place respectively in the center-city market share of more than $2 billion in retail sales.[14] Both stores conducted extensive renovation and expansion of product lines in the wake of the Faneuil Hall project. Jordan Marsh completed a $30-million renovation of its downtown store ` which stresses its soft lines, while Filene's expanded into the home furnishings division.[15]

While the renovation of the Boston center city has created a new arena for retail competition, it has also attracted potential customers for other urban stores. The Newbury Street shopping district with its

Lord & Taylor, Saks 5th Avenue, and Louis', is also oriented toward the upper-income urban consumer, but the boom may be coming to an end in Boston. As an industry spokesman put it,[16]

> *At some time the bubble has to burst. Regardless of the disposable income here, there isn't the sophisticated purchasing you have in New York or Palm Beach. This is old Yankee money. They don't spend the principal, just the interest.*

All of these developments in the specialty mode should not be confused with the traditional ownership pattern in this segment of the retail market. The character of this mode in its current reincarnation is quite different from that of a hundred years ago. Specialty stores are now not necessarily privately owned independents. They are increasingly owned by large corporate entities which use them to penetrate markets otherwise unavailable to them. The same corporation can operate low-price discount outlets to take advantage of the suburban market and control downtown fashionable specialty shops to capture the urban retail dollar.

Methods of Expansion

In moving to the suburbs or expanding in the central city, retailers have relied on three strategies:

1. New construction and procurement of buildings vacated by firms that have gone out of business.
2. Acquisition of smaller firms, giving broader market representation or regional representation.
3. Expansion of product lines (that is, internal rather than geographical expansion).

The acquisition of vacant store sites as a substitute for new construction has become a cost-effective expansion strategy that has provided many firms with key locations in major markets. When W.T. Grant filed for bankruptcy under Chapter XI, several large chains expressed an active interest in bidding on Grant's locations. The same thing occurred when Arlan's, Interstate, Turnstyle, and J.M. Fields filed for bankruptcy. Some firms shy away from previously used sites, feeling that "customers in the area would associate them [the new companies] with a loser."[17] Others, however, feel that the savings accrued justify the extra hardship of overcoming the past association and that their corporate image will be strong enough to prevail against this liability.

Another method of expansion, particularly characteristic of corporate-owned holding companies, is the acquisition of "living" firms. Independent family-owned stores are often induced to sell to a holding company, relinquishing their autonomy in order to obtain help with financing and ease the severe cash-flow constraints that often plague them. Becoming part of a larger network may permit expansion which would otherwise have been prohibitively expensive. For example, G. Fox of Hartford, Connecticut, was able to expand to the suburbs, using cash made available to it by the May Company when it became part of this national holding company.

A merger may also offer to a small company managerial resources and economies of scale. Moreover, a family may sell their business simply because they are tired of minding the store or because they would prefer not to have all of their financial assets tied up in a single business. Charles Lazarus, founder of the successful Toys Я Us, sold his business to Interstate in order to realize a capital gain, but received the option to retain managerial control.

The motivations for a large department or discount chain to merge into a still larger organization are more varied. Like a small independent, a chain acquired by a larger company can benefit from improved economies of scale and the greater resources of a broader financial network. A $500-million business like Bradlees, for instance, benefits from the size and solid reputation of its $2 billion parent company, Stop & Shop. Industry sources maintain that Mobil brought to Montgomery-Ward an established reputation for solid long-range planning, an area of reported weakness at Ward's. The management of Ward's also felt that although in the short run they would not receive any new capital from Mobil, the simple fact of their association with the oil giant would provide increased credibility for the department store chain in its dealings with real estate brokers, banks, suppliers, and prospective managerial talent. One Ward's executive who favored acquisition argued that, "the fact that Mobil is there may help us get into shopping centers. Developers that haven't been interested in us may think differently now."[18]

There are, however, reasons other than a financially inadequate offer that discourage firms from selling out. Private owners face the loss of managerial autonomy when they concede to a bid by a possible buyer, and for all managers—from the small entrepreneur to the corporate president—the loss of control over a store's management is an unattractive prospect. Managers may be uncertain about how the new parent company will treat its acquisition. Said a Ward's vice-president of the Mobil buy-out:[19]

We wondered if we would get the mushroom treatment. First they [the new owners] put you in the dark. Then they cover you with manure. Then they cultivate you. Then they let you steam for awhile. Finally, they can you.

Although the benefits of being part of the financial network of a larger company generally outweigh considerations of this sort, mergers may have financial disadvantages, too. One department store executive complained that the holding company of which his store was a part has siphoned profits generated locally and reinvested them in the Sunbelt. Still, the same holding company had provided some of the capital which had enabled the New England store to prosper and expand in the past. There were very real disadvantages, he said, in being part of a larger operation, but he conceded that his enterprise would probably have fared worse in the capital market without a strong parent company.

A profitable department store may expand through internal growth or diversification in its product line. Like many other big discounters, once K-Mart had established itself financially, it began buying out the specialty companies which previously leased departments in its various stores. In 1967 Holly Stores, principal licensee for women's and children's clothing, was purchased outright by K-Mart. In a later year, a licensee operating forty-two sporting goods departments was also acquired. Such acquisitions increase corporate profitability because they allow the parent company to realize profits which originally went to the licensee. Other stores like Filene's have diversified into new product lines in order to garner a larger share of the overall retail market. Still other firms have used "surplus" profits to enter totally different businesses.

Retail Expansion into Nonretail Areas

The expansion of retail firms into nonretail areas is fast becoming a common phenomenon. One of the first such diversifications, the entry of Sears into the insurance business through its subsidiary, the Allstate Insurance Company, has met with tremendous success. A few major chains have followed suit with insurance acquisitions, like the 1974 purchase of Planned Marketing Associates by K-Mart. T.J. Newton, Jr. of Blyth Eastman Dillon & Company points out that insurance companies are attractive acquisitions for a wide variety of companies because of . . . their relative immunity to the business cycle, their strong balance sheets, their capital-generating ability, and the straight-forward nature of their assets—bonds, stocks, and mortgages rather than plant and equipment.[20] Besides providing opportunities for increasing profits, insurance companies may also be helpful in easing a corporation's cash-flow problems.

Expansion into real estate has proven to be a natural extension of the department store business. All stores own or lease their buildings, and many build some or all of their own plants; thus, department store chains learn the real estate business by necessity. Moreover, with the suburbanization of retail trade, department stores have become involved in the establishment of regional and local shopping centers. In so doing, some department store chains—especially the larger ones—became developers as well as tenants. Homart, a Sears real-estate development subsidiary, is heavily involved in regional shopping centers. K-Mart, by contrast, builds relatively few of its own stores, and then only in order to be able to check the cost-effectiveness of its construction subcontractors. Even independent Grover-Cronin, despite its small size, pays rent on its own building to its affiliate, Grover-Cronin Realty Company.

Just as there is some integration between the modes of production (for example, holding companies owning both discount and conventional department stores), there is also a degree of vertical integration between wholesalers, retailers, and manufacturers. A few retailers, particularly the largest corporate concerns, have partially or completely bought out their merchandise suppliers. Sears was the leader in this field. Early in its history it was active in acquiring full or partial interest in its suppliers in order to ensure an adequate supply of goods at a favorable price. K-Mart, however, has taken the opposite tack, avoiding outright ownership of its suppliers because it prefers to be free to purchase where the price is best. Also, K-Mart's policy is to avoid the Sears emphasis on private labels, believing that name brands at reasonable prices are a major source of the store's appeal. So far K-Mart's only manufacturing tie is an interest in a subsidiary of the Melville Shoe Corporation.

It is also not unusual for retailers to venture into wholesale distribution. Caldor now owns several highly successful subsidiaries including Admore Distributors, Inc., a full-line sporting goods distributor; Leisure Line Toys, Inc., a distributor of toys and other related leisure products; and Ralar Distributors, Inc., a distributor of hardware, housewares, and garden equipment. But acquisition, of course, goes in the opposite direction as well—from manufacturer to retailer.

Expansion of Nonretail Firms into Retail Areas

In recent years department stores have proved an attractive acquisition for firms outside the retail sector. Shoe companies in particular, long the suppliers or lessees of department stores, began buying out department stores when foreign imports began to pose a serious threat to their survival as manufacturers. During the past two decades, Genesco purchased Bonwit Teller in New York, U.S. Shoe purchased Casual Corner, and Melville Shoe purchased Marshall's. It seems likely that as manufacturing opportunities shrink—at least in the United States—companies whose primary base is in manufacturing may shift their domestic operations in the direction of retail trade.

An analogous movement is visible in the extraction industries. Well-established department and discount concerns are particularly vulnerable to takeover if the price/earnings ratio of their stock is low. In such cases a high-growth firm with an inflated price/earnings ratio can effect a takeover with relative ease through an exchange of stock. Citing diminishing domestic supplies of oil, an industry observer said, "They can't keep their operations happy picking over the United States, so oil companies will reach out in order not to expire."[21] Mobil Oil's 1976 acquisition of Montgomery Ward may turn out to be only the first such move. Rawleigh Warner, Jr., Mobil's chief executive notes that "one of the things that attracted us to Marcor [Montgomery Ward and its partner, Container Corporation of America] was the steps Ward's had taken to effect a comeback," while its depressed prices showed that "Wall Street hadn't recognized the progress they'd made."[22]

Although the fortunes of individual firms may rise and fall, the retail sector is still viewed by industry executives as a relatively stable, safe investment because they believe the level of consumption in the United States "appears as if it is here to stay."[23] Despite highly publicized business failures and heavy competition in the industry, investors seem to view retail as a growth industry, particularly in the discount field and in areas, such as pharmaceuticals, which have not been thoroughly penetrated by mass merchandising. Whether this continues to be true in an age of growing saturation remains to be seen.

Expansion into Foreign Markets

One response by U.S. retail firms to apparent diminishing returns offered in domestic markets has been expansion into foreign coun-

tries. As with national expansion, international penetration is financially feasible for only large and profitable firms. American department stores have sold their wares abroad since at least 1945, when a
major general merchandise store established a wholly owned subsidiary in Mexico. Expansion to overseas retail markets (primarily
Europe, Canada, South America, and even Japan) can assume a
variety of forms:

1. Establishment of a wholly owned subsidiary.
2. Creation of a partial or co-equal ownership of a subsidiary.
3. Representation through an agency, agent relationship, or sales
    office abroad.

Catalog and mail-order sales are popular ways of doing business
because of the small initial investments required, but direct ownership of a subsidiary is the most prevalent form of overseas expansion. Sears has approximately 90 retail stores in 10 Latin American
countries; Simpson-Sears, Ltd., a 50-percent-owned affiliate, operates 28 retail stores and 345 catalog sales outlets throughout
Canada.[24]

Overseas expansion involves a geographic shift of capital from the
domestic market to a foreign economy. In this respect the capital
movements of the retail trade sector are following the patterns which
occurred a generation ago in the extraction and manufacturing industries. Multi-national department store trade will prosper in locations
where affluent manufacturing, extraction, and service industries are
located.

The development of the national holding company and enormous
chains like K-Mart has therefore radically changed the investment
structure of the industry. Much like firms in the manufacturing
sector, department stores have become increasingly footloose as new
forms of ownership make possible the rapid reallocation of capital
resources from one region to another and from retail trade to other
industrial sectors. This type of locational flexibility on the part of
corporate retail enterprises poses serious problems for individual
communities trying to hold onto their employment base. It is particularly worrisome for the regions approaching retail saturation, for even
minor losses in profit levels if sustained for any period of time can be
sufficient to induce central office managers to consider disinvestment
or other forms of capital transfer away from the region. The demise of
the private independent retailer is, consequently, an ominous sign for
those who support local control of a community's economic base.

Endnotes

1. Eleanore Carruth, "K-Mart Has to Open Some New Doors on the Future," *Fortune* (July 1977), p. 144.
2. "Saving the Company that Acquired Him," *Business Week* (February 19, 1979), p. 48.
3. "Shifting Gears with $18b Sears," *Boston Globe* (February 18, 1979).
4. Steven H. Star, "Sears, Roebuck and Co." (Boston, Mass.: Harvard Business School, Intercollegiate Case Clearing House, No. 6-570-040: M 386, 1969), p. 12.
5. Carruth, *op. cit.*, p. 146.
6. "Federated . . . and the Consumer Comeback," *Dun's Review* (December 1967), p. 38.
7. Robert Lenzer, "Massive Shakeup Yields Dividend," *Boston Globe* (April 12, 1979).
8. "70's—A Decade for Individuality," *Discount Store News*, Vol. 11, No. 26 (December 11, 1972), p. 47.
9. Carruth, *op. cit.*, p. 147.
10. "Retail Heavies Struggle in the Hub," *Boston Globe* (April 1, 1979), p. 27.
11. *Ibid.*
12. Carrie Tuhy, "Boston: An Old Grey Lady Finds the Secret of Youth," *Daily News Record* (March 1979), p. 7.
13. *Ibid.*, p. 15.
14. *Ibid.*
15. *Ibid.*
16. *Ibid.*
17. "President's Survey—Review of a Rough Year and Prospects for 1975," *Discount Merchandiser* (December 1974), p. 25.
18. "Big Oil's Move into Retailing," *Chain Store Age Executive* (September 1976), p. 31.
19. *Ibid.*, p. 30.
20. Robert J. Cole, "Prime Takeover Target: Insurance Companies," *The New York Times* (May 29, 1979), p. D1.
21. "Big Oil's Move into Retailing," *Chain Store Age Executive*, p. 32.
22. *Ibid.*
23. U.S. Bureau of Economic Analysis, *Survey of Current Business* (August 1973 and April 1974).
24. Gordon E. Miracle, "Sears, Roebuck and Company, Brazil (A)" Boston, Mass.: Harvard Business School, Intercollegiate Case Clearing House, No. 9-572-624 (1971), p. 1.

Selected Sources

"Big Oil's Move into Retailing," *Chain Store Age Executive* (September 1976), p. 31.
Carruth, Eleanore, "K-Mart Has to Open Some New Doors on the Future," *Fortune* (July, 1977), p. 44.

"President's Survey—Review of a Rough Year and Prospects for 1975," *Discount Merchandiser* (December 1974), p. 33.

"Retail Heavies Struggle in the Hub," *Boston Globe* (April 1, 1979), p. 27.

"Saving the Company that Acquired Him," *Business Week* (February 19, 1979), p. 48.

"70's—A Decade for Individuality," *Discount Store News*, Vol. II, No. 26 (December 11, 1972), p. 47.

Tuhy, Carrie, "Boston: An Old Grey Lady Finds the Secret of Youth," *Daily News Record* (March 1970), p. 7.

Chapter 5

THE DEPARTMENT STORE LABOR FORCE: TRENDS, TURNOVER, AND TENURE

Industrial transformation as profound as that in retail trade could not have occurred without dramatic changes in the structure of the labor force. Recruiting workers to fill the millions of new clerk, warehouse, buyer, and manager positions was a monumental task in itself. It required a restructuring of the workplace and extraordinary modifications in the actual methods of retailing merchandise. All of this was part of a retail revolution which saw the industry take advantage of a growing army of unskilled young workers and a generation of women ready to return to the labor market. There are few instances in modern employment history—besides World War II—that compare to this mobilization.

Employment figures tell a good part of the story by themselves. About 6.5 million workers were employed in retail trade in 1947. Of these, about 11 percent (or 700,000) were working in department stores. For every 100 workers employed in manufacturing, 212 were employed in occupations related to retailing. By 1980 the retail ranks had swollen to nearly 15 million, a net average addition of over a quarter million workers each year. For every 100 in manufacturing, there are now over 250 in trade.[1] Despite radical changes in retail methods, a significant shift has occurred in the labor needed to sell merchandise in contrast to that needed to produce it.

Demand for labor has closely followed the fortunes of the industry. Saturation in the marketplace translates into stagnation or decline in employment, as data for New England clearly indicate. Once again

New England serves as a good example because it has led the nation in the evolution of the industry.

During most of the 1960's, when New England employment was eroding in the traditional nondurable manufacturing sector—with enormous downslides in apparel, textiles, and footwear—the retail trade and service industries were booming. They were responsible for creating hundreds of thousands of jobs which kept the jobless rate from rising higher than the alarming 12–15 percent experienced by old mill towns such as Fall River and New Bedford, Massachusetts.

Department stores played a major role in this expansion. The number of employees in this sector of the retail market grew by an annual average of nearly 8.6 percent, leaping from fewer than 90,000 in 1958 to a peak of 204,000 a decade later.* The annual rate of growth was almost four times the average for all New England industries. It was clearly the heyday of the department store.

Most of this job creation coincided with the 1970's consumer boom and the rapid proliferation of the suburban shopping mall and the discount store. Indeed, more than 70 percent of the expansion occurred in just four years—1964 to 1968—as stores sprang up everywhere. Yet nearly as quickly as the boom started in New England, it ceased. Even two years *before* the 1971 recession, employment had

---

*These statistics and others in this chapter are based, unless otherwise noted, on special tabulations of a unique data source: the Social Security Administration's (SSA) Longitudinal Employer-Employee Data (LEED) File. This file contains information on a one percent sample of all workers covered by the Social Security system and includes a complete work history for each individual for the period 1957–1975. These special tabulations were prepared at the Social Welfare Research Institute at Boston College.

The LEED data include all workers who worked *at any time* during the year in the industry and therefore enumerate a larger number of workers in each industry than job "slots." This is particularly true in high-turnover industries such as department stores. A comparison of LEED employment with County Business Pattern data suggests that on average there are between two and three times as many employees during the year as there are employees listed in the mid-March CBP counts. The ratio is significantly higher in years in which there were net growth.

New England Department Store Industry (SIC 531)

Year	LEED	CBP	Ratio
1959	92,100	42,260	2.17
1965	153,600	55,415	2.77
1968	204,100	72,090	2.83
1971	165,200	80,825	2.04
1975	175,000	84,042	2.08

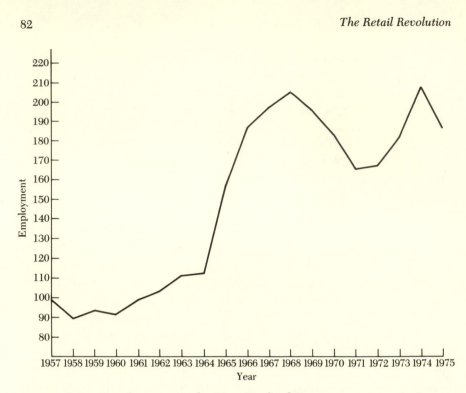

Figure 5.1. Employment in the New England Department Store Industry, 1957–1975 (in thousands). (*Source: LEED file analysis*).

begun a precipitous decline, falling by 40,000 from the 1968 peak (See Figure 5.1).

Part of the employment crash was related to the recession, but much more of it can be traced to the industry shake-out which was inevitable, regardless of overall economic trends. The expansion had been too rapid, given underlying consumer demand. As a result, the number of workers in this sector is no longer on the rise (in saturated New England), but instead exhibits a cyclical pattern consistent with the peaks and valleys of the overall economy. Employment continues to rise in other regions, but generally not at the pace of retail's golden decade.

Part-Time Employment

To be sure, part of the remarkable growth that occurred during the 1960's is illusory. Before the rise of the discount chain, department stores employed a much higher proportion of skilled full-time salespeople. Since then, the movement toward part-time employment has swelled the official employment numbers. In 1963, for example, nonsupervisory employees worked an average of 34.1 hours per week; by 1973 average weekly hours had declined to 31.4.

When these national averages (extrapolated to 1959 and 1976) are applied to the New England *County Business Patterns* employment scene, and use is made of the industry's own 40-hour week "census unit" which defines full-time equivalent (FTE) employment, FTE expansion is found to be 67 percent. While this is substantial, it is far lower than the reported job growth of 91 percent over the 1959 to 1976 period.

New England, as a leader in the discount business, leads the nation in the trend toward part-time work. Local industry sources suggest that 75 percent of all department store employees are now part-time. One large, regionally based discount chain goes so far as to suggest that only 15 percent of its labor force is employed on a full-time schedule. Extended store hours dictate the use of part-timers, industry sources claim. Full-time schedules are seen as inefficient as they allegedly fail to provide sufficient flexibility to store managers in their attempts to cover peak selling hours.

Seasonal labor provides additional flexibility in scheduling the industry's workforce. The numbers suggest seasonality every bit as severe as agricultural employment, with part-year workers being used to meet peak season demand. On average, only about one out of three (35 percent) department store employees work year-round. At the other end of the spectrum, a larger number (38 percent) work one quarter or less during the year, most during the busy Christmas season. These temporary schedules are concentrated among young workers with 63 percent of all those under age 25 employed no more than three months out of the year. Many of these are high school and college students who work during the Christmas season or during summer vacations. In contrast, only 17 percent of those employees age 25–34 worked this little, and only 15 percent among those age 35–54.

As the industry moves toward part-time and seasonal work, the whole complexion of the labor force is changing. No longer does the industry draw significant numbers of its workers from among those who expect long-term employment at a salary adequate for a household head. The emergence of a large group of women and youths who will accept part-time work at the minimum wage has permitted a dramatic change in the department store industry's use of labor. It shows up in turnover and tenure, in the age structure of the work-force, and in the sources the industry draws upon to replace depart-ing workers and hire new workers for expansion.

Turnover and Tenure in the Labor Force

Few industries have employee-separation rates as high as department stores. Rather than a permanent occupation, today retail trade pro-vides most of its younger workers with a way-station in their careers. For some it is an introduction to the world of work; for other workers it is a supplement to a regular full-time job. That is not how it has always been. An analysis of the New England LEED file confirms a distinct drop in job permanency within the industry.

According to LEED, during the 1950's, 42 percent of the total workforce had three or more continuous years of employment in the industry. By the 1960's this proportion fell to 35 percent, and during the 1970's to 32 percent. Over the same period of time, those spend-ing one year or less in the industry went from 19 percent of the total workforce to 27 percent (see Table 5.1).

From the perspective of the personnel director, the turnover rate is a staggering challenge. For example, if one traces the tenure of everyone in the industry in 1968, over half of the labor force is found to have left their jobs by the end of 1969 and nearly four out of five by 1971. By 1975 only one in twelve of the original workforce is still employed in the industry (see Table 5.2). Some of these workers retired, became disabled, or died, while others were fired or laid off and did not return to the industry. But by far most of the turnover was due to "voluntary quits" by workers who never intended the job to be permanent or who found that the industry paid too little to warrant permanent employment.

With fewer than one new hire out of three remaining for more than a year in the industry and the overall separation rate running as high as 50 percent per year, new hiring must proceed at a frantic pace even

Table 5.1.   **Turnover in the Department Store Industry, 1950's–1970's**

	% Working at Least 3 Years	% Working 1 Year or Less
1950's	42.4	18.9
1960's	34.7	25.1
1970's	31.7	27.0

SOURCE: LEED special tabulation.

Table 5.2. Tenure in the Department Store Industry (Origin = 1968)

	% Male	*% Female*	*Total %*
0–1 Year or less	52.7	47.6	49.3
0–2 Years or less	73.0	68.7	70.2
0–3 Years or less	79.5	78.1	78.6
Still in SIC 531 in 1975	9.5	8.5	8.8

SOURCE: LEED special tabulation.

during recessions. This is the reason why help-wanted advertisements appear virtually all the time in the industry. The pace of new hiring has had to be accelerated as the rate of turnover has increased.

Table 5.3 illustrates this phenomenon by breaking down the annual net change in New England employment into "gross separations" and "gross accessions." The former includes lay-offs, voluntary quits, and dismissals, while the latter covers new hires and rehires. Note that the separation rate has risen from 36 to 41 percent (excluding 1957–1958) during the late 1950's and early 1960's, to the 42-to-51-percent range by the mid–1970's. The sheer numbers are extraordinary in themselves, reaching over 100,000 separations a year in the six New

Table 5.3. Separation and Accession Rates in New England Department Stores, 1957–1975

Turnover Year	*Gross Separations*	*%*	*Gross Accessions*	*%*	*Net Δ*
1957–1958	43,900	(45.1)	36,400	(37.4)	−7,500
1958–1959	31,900	(35.5)	34,200	(38.1)	2,300
1959–1960	36,500	(39.6)	35,800	(38.9)	−700
1960–1961	33,400	(36.5)	40,700	(44.5)	7,300
1961–1962	37,400	(37.9)	50,100	(50.8)	12,700
1962–1963	44,300	(39.8)	52,600	(47.2)	8,300
1963–1964	50,100	(41.9)	51,200	(42.8)	1,100
1964–1965	49,300	(40.8)	82,100	(68.0)	32,800
1965–1966	64,600	(42.1)	96,900	(63.1)	32,300
1966–1967	83,100	(44.7)	93,700	(50.4)	10,600
1967–1968	87,900	(44.7)	95,500	(48.6)	7,600
1968–1969	100,700	(49.3)	92,600	(45.4)	−8,100
1969–1970	93,600	(47.8)	77,800	(39.7)	−15,800
1970–1971	84,800	(47.1)	69,800	(38.7)	−15,000
1971–1972	68,800	(41.6)	72,200	(43.7)	3,400
1972–1973	83,300	(49.4)	95,200	(56.5)	21,900
1973–1974	91,100	(50.5)	120,700	(66.9)	29,600
1974–1975	98,600	(46.9)	63,500	(30.2)	−35,100

SOURCE: LEED file analysis.

Table 5.4. **New England Department Store Average Separation and Accession Rates, 1957–1975**

	During Net Declines	During Net Increases
Average Separation Rate	46.0%	42.1%
Average Accession Rate	38.4%	51.7%

England states alone. It was necessary to hire over 92,000 in 1969 to keep the net decline in employment to 8,100. Clearly this is an industry in which the labor market is constantly churning with workers flooding in and out of the sector.

When all of this employment activity shakes out, the result is net expansion or contraction in the industry. The "gross flow" data help to explain how this occurs. During years of new employment gain, the gross separation rate averaged 42.1 percent.* (See Table 5.4.) One would expect this to be predominantly voluntary quits rather than lay-offs. Yet during periods of net decline in the industry, such as 1968 through 1971, the rate averaged only four percentage points higher.

These data can mean only that expansion and contraction in the industry is accomplished primarily by firms varying the number of new workers hired each year. There appear to be few lay-offs (except for seasonal reasons), for attrition is normally more than sufficient to allow for industry contraction. The managerial goal of maintaining an optimal level of employment rests on hiring a sufficient number of workers to cover attrition and any needed growth. Even in the 1975 recession when net employment in New England plummeted by 35,000, nearly 64,000 new workers had to be hired to compensate for a loss of more than 98,000. This is the nature of the industry. Such remarkably low, and decreasing, employment tenure could be tolerated only in an industry in which skill requirements for most jobs are minimal. While the necessity of replacing up to half the workforce in any given year imposes significant costs on the industry, the costs would be far greater if more firm-specific skill training were required. Given the high rate of turnover, department store firms have a strong incentive to keep skill requirements to a minimum; at the same time, the firm's decision to reduce skill requirements, pay only minimum wage, and tolerate increased turnover in the labor force makes jobs in this industry far less attractive to those workers who might otherwise choose to remain.

*Gross separation rate$_t$ = number of separations$_t$/total employment$_t$
 Gross accession rate$_t$ = number of accessions$_t$/total employment$_t$

Table 5.5. Origin of Department Store Employees (Destination: 1974)

Origin 1973	% of Total (Total = 210,100)	% of Accessions (Total = 120,700)
Origin in SIC 531 in Region	42.6	—
Origin in SIC 531—Outside Region	1.6	2.7
Not In Covered Employment (NICE)	12.9	22.5
Military/Reserves	.5	.9
Unknown	5.2	9.0
Primary Sector	12.1	21.2
Secondary Sector	25.1	43.7
Top 5 Industries		
SIC 54 Food Stores	8.6	14.9
SIC 58 Eating & Drinking Places	3.6	6.3
SIC 53 General Merchandise Stores	3.1	5.4
SIC 56 Apparel & Accessory Stores	2.1	3.7
SIC 50 Wholesale Trade	1.7	3.0

SOURCE: LEED file analysis.

The Origin of the Workforce

The LEED file provides a clue to the source of this large new labor force. It is possible, for example, to trace the "origins" of the 1974 department store workforce by asking what these workers were doing in 1973. Table 5.5 shows that only 43 percent of those employed in New England department stores (SIC 531) in 1974 had been employed in this same industry in the region during the previous year. That is, of the 210,000 employees in the industry in 1974, only 89,400 were there in 1973. The remaining 120,700 had to be attracted to the industry.

Of these 120,000 new hires, a little more than one-fifth (22.5 percent) came from outside the covered labor force (Not In Covered Employment). Most of these were either working at their first job or were returning to the workforce after an employment hiatus. Another fifth transferred from "primary" sector jobs—jobs primarily in durable manufacturing and the higher wage services, while two-fifths came out of "secondary" sector industries—nondurable manufacturing, retail trade, and the lower-wage services. Consequently more than three out of five of the new department store employees came from outside the labor force altogether or from other low-wage sectors. This is confirmed by the list of industries which provide the largest numbers of workers to department stores. More than 20

percent of the new workforce transferred from food stores, res-
taurants, taverns, and bars, while close to another 10 percent came
from other branches of retail trade. Mobility from the usually higher-
wage primary sector contributes comparatively few workers to the
department store industry. *In the short-run,* workers appear to shift
around in fairly well-defined orbits rather than across industrial sectors. The high degree of short-term inter-industry mobility does not
appear to imply an equally high amount of "upward" mobility. For all
the churning and tumult in these markets, there is surprising stability
within broad industry groups.

Within all this labor activity, there are significant differences in the
labor force origins of men and women (see Table 5.6). Over one-
fourth of the women who joined the department store workforce in
1974 had no (covered) employment experience at all in the previous
year. Men were much more likely to have worked in another industry
in 1973, and only one-sixth were out of the labor force. Men were also
much more likely to have origins in the primary sector, although
approximately equal proportions (two out of five) of men and women

Table 5.6.   Origin of Department Store Employees by Sex (Destination: 1974)

	Percentage of Accessions		
	Total (120,700)	Men (43,800)	Women (76,000)
Origin 1973			
Origin in SIC 531 in Region	—	—	—
Origin in SIC 531—Outside Region	2.7	1.8	3.3
Not In Covered Employment (NICE)	22.5	16.7	25.9
Military & Reserves	.9	2.5	0
Unknown	9.0	5.5	11.1
Primary Sector	21.2	27.2	17.2
Secondary Sector	43.7	46.3	42.5

Top 5 Industries

Men			Women		
SIC 54	Food Stores	19.6	SIC 54	Food Stores	12.2
SIC 58	Eating & Drinking	6.8	SIC 58	Eating & Drinking	6.2
SIC 50	Wholesale Trade	4.6	SIC 53	General	6.1
SIC 53	General	4.1		Merchandise	
	Merchandise		SIC 56	Apparel &	4.7
SIC 55	Automotive Dealers	2.5		Accessory Stores	
	& Gasoline Sta-		SIC 60	Health Services	3.0
	tions				

SOURCE: LEED file analysis.

came from other secondary sector jobs. Still this does not alter the general conclusion that department store workers, despite the enormous short-term turnover, usually begin and end up someplace in the trade sector. The movement, for example, between food stores and department stores is quite common, especially for men.

The Destination of the Labor Force

Tracing labor-force origins tells something about the new recruits to the industry, but what happens to all those who leave this sector each year? Where do they go and how do they fare? Table 5.7 traces the 1975 destination of New England department store employees who worked in the industry sometime during 1974. Of the 210,000 employees, only a little over half (53 percent) were still employed in the industry within the region one year later. Another 1.1 percent (2,100) remained in the industry, but had moved outside the region. All the rest left the industry.

Of those who left, about one in twenty retired, died, or became disabled while another 2 percent joined the military. A much larger proportion—nearly one in five—departed altogether from the labor

Table 5.7. Destination of Department Store Employees, All Employees (Origin: 1974)

Destination: 1975	% of Total (Total = 210,100)	% of Separations (Total = 98,600)
Remain in SIC 531 in Region	53.1	—
Remain in SIC 531—Out of Region	1.1	2.4
Not In Covered Employment (NICE)	9.2	19.7
Retired, Disabled, Deceased, Other NICE	2.4	5.2
Military/Reserves	.9	1.9
Unknown	1.3	2.8
Primary Sector	15.8	33.8
Secondary Sector	16.1	34.2
Top 5 Industries		
SIC 58 Eating & Drinking Places	2.9	6.2
SIC 80 Health Services	2.7	5.8
SIC 59 Miscellaneous Retail	1.8	3.9
SIC 54 Food Stores	1.6	3.4
SIC 90 Government Services	1.6	3.4

SOURCE: LEED file analysis.

force (or found work in noncovered jobs). The remaining two-thirds who took their leave from department store jobs found work in other industries, dividing about equally between primary and secondary sectors. Still, the industries that claimed the largest number of mobile workers were generally in the secondary sector. Apparently sales clerks left in significant numbers to become waiters and waitresses, nurses aides and orderlies, and check-out workers in grocery stores.

There is indeed a vital difference in mobility according to the age of the workforce (see Tables 5.8 and 5.9). As noted previously, most young workers stay in the industry for only a brief spell. Among workers under twenty-five, only two out of five remain in the employ of a department store for more than a year. In contrast, seven out of ten workers aged 35–54 do so. The younger group, however, moves on to other jobs more often than their older counterparts. Over a third of the 35–54 age group leave the covered labor force within a year, the overwhelming majority (90%) of these being middle-aged women. Only 13 percent of the younger group are found outside of the covered labor force after they leave their department store employers.

Age is also a primary determinant of the types of jobs these mobile workers obtain when they leave. Those in the younger group who

Table 5.8.   Destination of Department Store Employees, Age < 25 (Origin: 1974)

Destination: 1975	% of Total (Total = 110,900)	% of Separations (Total = 65,200)
Remain in SIC 531 in Region	41.2	—
Remain in SIC 531—Out of Region	.7	1.2
Not In Covered Employment (NICE)	7.7	13.0
Retired, Disabled, Deceased, Other NICE	2.7	4.6
Military/Reserves	1.4	2.5
Unknown	1.3	2.1
Primary Sector	21.6	36.7
Secondary Sector	23.4	39.9
Top 5 Industries		
SIC 58 Eating & Drinking Places	4.4	7.5
SIC 80 Health Services	3.9	6.6
SIC 60 Miscellaneous Retail	2.8	4.8
SIC 54 Food Stores	2.3	3.8
SIC 90 Government Service	2.2	3.7

SOURCE: LEED file analysis.

Table 5.9. Destination of Department Store Employees, Age 35–54 (Origin: 1974)

Destination: 1975	% of Total (Total = 43,500)	% of Separations (Total = 12,100)
Remain in SIC 531 in Region	> 2.2	—
Remain in SIC 531—Out of Region	2.3	8.3
Not In Covered Employment (NICE)	9.9	35.5
Retired, Disabled, Deceased, Other NICE	.5	1.7
Military/Reserves	.2	.8
Unknown	1.1	4.1
Primary Sector	12.6	45.4
Secondary Sector	3.7	13.2
Top 5 Industries		
SIC 80 Health Services	1.1	4.1
SIC 36 Electrical Equipment Manufacturing	.9	3.3
SIC 90 Government Service	.7	2.5
SIC 54 Food Stores	.7	2.5
SIC 58 Eating & Drinking Places	.7	2.5

SOURCE: LEED file analysis.

remain working find jobs more often than not in other secondary sector industries, while more than three out of four of the middle-aged group end up, or more correctly return, to primary sector jobs in such industries as electrical equipment manufacture and government service. This is particularly true of men.

When added together, these statistics seem to suggest the various roles department stores now play in the American labor market. This $90-billion industry is increasingly responsible for providing part-time jobs for those in school, similar to the sorts of "pocket-money" job opportunities offered by grocery stores, restaurants, and other secondary employers. Moreover, for many women over the age of 25, the retail sector has become a place for periodic employment. For some men in this age group it provides temporary jobs when they are laid off from their normal employers, or when they or their families require a second source of earnings. "Moonlighting" is quite common among workers in this sector. For very few workers does this major industry provide stable career jobs. Consequently, creation of department store slots can hardly serve to offset losses in the manufacturing sector. This may indeed be a sobering conclusion for those who would look to this sector as a source of economic development in the "mature" regions of the country.

But before concluding on such a pessimistic note, it is useful to

Table 5.10. Industry Origin and Destination of All Department Store Employees in New England, 1974

| | % of Inter-Industry Transfers | |
	Origin	Destination
Primary Sector	32.7	49.7
Secondary Sector	67.3	50.3

SOURCE: LEED file analysis.

compare the "origin" and "destination" statistics that have been presented. The numbers indicate that emanating from this constant flux in employment there is some "upward" mobility, after all, from the secondary to the primary sector. New employees in the department store industry are more likely to come from the secondary sector, while those who leave the industry for other employment have an even chance of landing a job in a primary firm. Thus for some workers the department store appears to be a way-station to what can be presumed "better" employment (see Table 5.10). This holds true for both men and women (see Table 5.11).

Long-Run Trends in Labor Mobility

That department stores play the role of a way-station for some workers in the industry is also substantiated by looking at longer-run labor mobility channels. Instead of looking at one-year transitions, one can follow inter-industry changes over a number of years. Tables 5.12 and 5.13 do this by providing information on the labor market destinations of those employed in the industry over a seven-year period. The first table covers 1958–1965, while the latter looks at a comparable span a decade later.

According to the data, young people simply do not remain in the industry. Among those under twenty-five, only one in twenty (5.8

Table 5.11. Industry Origin and Destination of Department Store Employees by Sex in New England, 1974

| | % Men | | % Women | |
	Origin	Destination	Origin	Destination
Primary	38.3	54.8	28.8	45.9
Secondary	61.7	45.2	71.2	54.1

SOURCE: LEED file analysis.

Table 5.12. **Destination of Department Store Employees, Age Cohort 1958 (Origin: 1958/Destination: 1965)**

Destination: 1965	% < 25 (Total = 27,800)	% 25–34 (Total = 13,000)	% 35–54 (Total = 34,000)	% 55 + (Total = 15,000)
Remain in SIC 531 in Region	5.8	20.8	39.1	32.7
Remain in SIC 531—Out of Region	1.1	1.5	.6	—
Not In Covered Employment (NICE)	39.2	21.5	21.2	6.7
Retired, Disabled, Deceased, Other NICE	.4	1.5	4.7	46.7
Military/Reserves	5.0	.8	—	—
Unknown	—	—	—	—
Primary Sector	31.3	30.8	16.2	10.0
Secondary Sector	17.3	23.1	18.2	4.0

SOURCE: LEED file analysis.

Table 5.13. Destination of Department Store Employees, Age Cohort 1968 (Origin: 1968/Destination: 1975)

Destination: 1975	% < 25 (Total = 98,700)	% 25–34 (Total = 30,100)	% 35–54 (Total = 51,400)	% 55 + (Total = 23,900)
Remain in SIC 531 in Region	5.9	15.3	29.2	22.6
Remain in SIC 531—Out of Region	1.1	4.3	2.5	.4
Not In Covered Employment (NICE)	29.0	25.6	23.5	14.2
Retired, Disabled, Deceased, Other NICE	.7	1.3	3.7	50.6
Military/Reserves	2.3	1.7	.4	—
Unknown	1.1	1.0	.4	—
Primary Sector	39.3	28.8	20.0	5.0
Secondary Sector	20.6	21.9	20.0	7.1

SOURCE: LEED file analysis.

percent) remains as long as seven years. In the earlier period, before the well-recognized rise in female labor-force participation, about half of young employees found jobs in other sectors, while almost 40 percent left the covered labor force altogether. Among young women, more than half (54.7 percent) left the labor market, while among men less than 6 percent left. Ten years later, fewer than 30 percent were dropping out of the labor force, with the rate down to 36 percent for women. Meanwhile the same small percentage (5.9 percent) stayed in the industry. Of those few who did remain, young men were more likely to develop career patterns in the industry, presumably rising in the managerial hierarchy (see Chapter 6).

Mobility to the primary sector is clearly evident for those under 25. In both periods, young workers leaving the industry graduated to the primary sector in roughly twice the numbers as those who remained in secondary industries. Again, however, the differences between men and women are striking. The ratio of primary to secondary sector placements was over 3 to 1 for men in both periods, while it increased from only 1.1 to 1.4 for women. There is presumably some improvement here, but it remains slow as many studies of job segregation have repeatedly shown.

In comparison with the extremely high rates of mobility among young workers, those aged 25–34 are much less mobile. Yet even they are deserting the industry in larger numbers. The proportion remaining as department store employees declined from 20.8 percent to 15.3 percent over the two seven-year periods. The decline among workers aged 35–54 was even steeper—from 39.1 to 29.2 percent. Given the part-time low-wage jobs now available in the industry, it appears that prime-age workers are finding it increasingly difficult to support families and are therefore transferring to other sectors. Unlike younger workers, their mobility seems much more restricted—with those 35–54 transferring to the primary sector in no greater numbers than those who remain in other secondary industries. The great upward mobility is apparently limited to the young—those who may not have intended to remain in the industry for long anyway.

What is then overwhelmingly clear—for every age group and for both men and women—is the declining permanency within the industry. This phenomenon, perhaps more than anything else, speaks to the fundamental transformation in the nature of this industry. Fewer workers consider the department store sector to offer a satisfactory career—with the presumable exception of those who obtain choice managerial slots. As a result, younger workers have grown literally to dominate the industry. By 1970 more than half of the

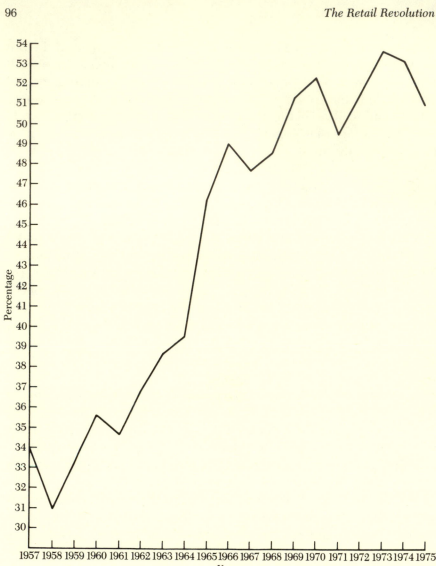

Figure 5.2. Percentage of Department Store Employees under Age 25. (*Source: LEED file analysis.*)

workforce was under 25, up from only 30 percent twelve years earlier (see Figure 5.2). For its own part, the industry has sought out this segment of the labor force so as to provide the flexibility the new industrial structure allegedly required and to reduce dependency on higher cost labor. In the course of this revolutionary transformation, the retail sector has lost its ability to provide regular career employ-ment for all but a handful of skilled managers. The days of the knowledgable career salesperson have given way to an era of check-out clerks who use the industry on a part-time basis to fill gaps in their income stream. This may be to the good of those who need or desire part-time periodic work, but the industry is no longer particularly helpful to those who are seeking steady employment and a career opportunity.

Endnote

1. U.S. Department of Labor, Bureau of Labor Statistics, *Employment and Earnings Statistics for the United States* (June 1980).

Chapter 6

EARNINGS, PRODUCTIVITY, AND THE NEW TECHNOLOGY OF RETAIL TRADE

Trends in the changing composition of the department store labor force are directly related to changes in the wages offered and the technology adopted by the industry. High wages attract certain types of labor as surely as low wages discourage others from ever applying. Technological advances in an industry can increase or decrease skill requirements and in so doing shape the labor force and the wage pattern.

In the case of department stores, the introduction of new sales technology has been instrumental in "deskilling" the labor force and has provided the industry with the ability to make ready use of inexperienced labor. Yet, at the other end of the spectrum, the transformation of the industry has made necessary the hiring of a whole new class of skilled technicians: white collar workers who manage the legal and accounting functions of modern corporate structures.

The combination of labor-saving merchandising techniques with hierarchical forms of management and control is responsible for generating a "dual labor market" within the industry. Within this structure are top management posts that bear every resemblance to the sophisticated supervisory positions in the traditional manufacturing sector. Below these few key job slots are the tens of thousands of low-wage jobs that provide the vast majority of employment opportunities in the industry.

Increasingly rare in this arrangement are the skilled sales jobs which at one time provided reasonable family incomes for a significant number of workers. For this reason, the industry is now best characterized as having a "missing middle." The modern department store—whether it be a part of a full-price or discount chain or a member of a national holding company—has a small number of high-salary opportunities and a sea of low-wage slots. In between are a rapidly diminishing number of skilled sales positions. Earnings data from the LEED file provide vivid illustrations of this fact.

Earnings in the Department Store Sector

Wage rates in retail trade are generally pegged to the legal minimum. As late as 1973, average hourly earnings were below $3.00, and even with double-digit price inflation wages averaged only $4.20 per hour in 1978. Average weekly earnings, shrunk even further by the preponderance of part-time work, fell to barely 60 percent of the average for all nonsupervisory employees in the economy, down from 67 percent only a decade earlier.

Men fared best in this market, but still averaged little more than $6,800 annually in 1975. Women, who make up most of the part-time labor force, earned only $2,800 (see Table 6.1). What is more, these figures—estimated from the New England LEED sample—do not include workers whose department store wages merely supplemented earnings from another job.

Statistics on average earnings, however, are quite deceptive, for they camouflage the substantial variation in earnings among age groups and can obscure basic wage-trends. This is particularly true in the retail sector where an employee's occupation is so closely linked to his or her age and sex. For example, in 1975, young men (under age 25) who worked year round (in four quarters, but not necessarily full-time) averaged $3,958.* Because of the reduction in average hours worked, this was actually no higher than the average earnings level in 1967 (see Table 6.2). Indeed, in inflation-adjusted dollars (1967 = 100), 1975 earnings represented more than a $1,500 drop in income, a reduction of over 38 percent (see Table 6.3).

In contrast, prime-age men (age 25–34) earned as much in department stores as the average for all other industries (except in 1975), and for men 35–54, real wage advances between 1957 and 1975 were actually more than double those for all industries taken together (see

---

*These figures do not include nonwhite minorities because the sample sizes of nonwhites disaggregated by age group are too small for statistical inference.

Table 6.1.   Annual Earnings (Current Dollars) of Primary Job Holders in Department Stores

	Men	Women
1957	$3,064	$1,353
1958	3,438	1,345
1959	3,676	1,334
1960	4,113	1,455
1961	4,371	1,515
1962	4,282	1,494
1963	4,301	1,498
1964	4,707	1,661
1965	3,962	1,626
1966	4,244	1,568
1967	4,654	1,765
1968	4,627	1,874
1969	5,081	2,002
1970	5,344	2,113
1971	5,921	2,220
1972	6,167	2,473
1973	6,293	2,352
1974	6,424	2,638
1975	6,811	2,834

SOURCE: LEED file analysis.

Table 6.2.   New England Department Store Industry Annual Earnings (Current Dollars) for Full-Year White Workers for Whom SIC 531 Was Primary Employer, by Age & Sex, 1962–1975

White Men	< 25	25–34	35–54	55 +
1962	2,263	5,994	7,481	7,511
1967	3,947	7,781	8,701	8,858
1972	3,772	9,393	13,223	11,216
1975	3,958	10,929	17,842	15,359

White Women	< 25	25–34	35–54	55 +
1962	1,950	3,962	2,654	2,517
1967	2,184	2,955	3,146	3,696
1972	2,627	4,104	4,019	4,367
1975	3,654	4,892	4,923	5,451

SOURCE: LEED file analysis.

Table 6.3.   Department Store Industry Real Wages (1967 = 100) for Full-Year White Workers for Whom SIC 531 Was Primary Employer, by Age and Sex, 1957–1975

White Men	< 25	25–34	35–54	55+
1957	2,763	6,395	5,933	7,750
1962	2,524*	6,686	8,345	8,378
1967	3,947	7,781	8,701	8,858
1972	2,968*	7,390	10,404	8,825
1975	2,442*	6,742*	11,007	9,475

White Women	< 25	25–34	35–54	55+
1957	2,103*	3,811	3,079	2,522*
1962	2,175*	4,419	2,960*	2,808*
1967	2,184*	2,955*	3,146*	3,696*
1972	2,067*	3,229*	3,162*	3,436*
1975	2,254*	3,018*	3,037*	3,363*

SOURCE: LEED file analysis.

* Earnings are statistically lower at the .05 level than the equivalent labor force for all industries.

Table 6.4). For this particular group, the department store became over the period of two decades an exceptionally good employer, paying nearly $18,000 a year in 1975—more than four times the rate paid the average young worker.

These large wage gains for what are mainly management personnel provide perhaps the most striking indication of a trend toward corporate hierarchical structure within the industry. Graphic evidence is

Table 6.4.   Percentage Real Wage Increase for Full-Year Primary Workers by Age, Race, and Sex, 1957–1975

White Men	< 25	25–34	35–54	55+
SIC 531	b	5.4	85.5	22.3
All Industries	18.0	32.4	41.4	27.0

White Women	< 25	25–34	35–54	55+
SIC 531	7.2	− 20.8	− 1.4	33.3
All Industries	− .1	25.3	21.2	32.5

SOURCE: LEED file analysis.

b sample size too small for statistical reliability.

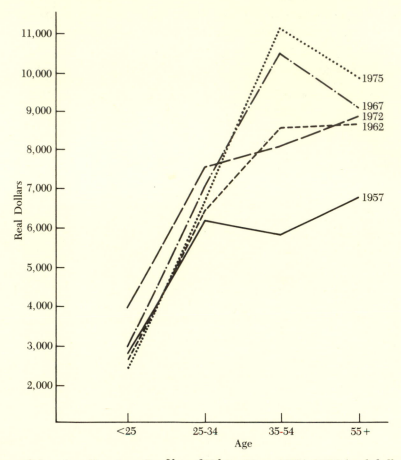

Figure 6.1.   Age Earnings Profiles of White Men, 1957–1975 (real dollars, 1967 = 100). (*Source: LEED file analysis.*)

provided by the age-earnings profile found in Figure 6.1, based on the data in Table 6.3. Before the explosive growth in large multi-unit establishments, the age-earnings profiles for men were relatively flat. This normally reflects the absence of internal job ladders and a relatively unbureaucratized, nonhierarchical form of management. It is fully consistent with the older style independent department store.

In more recent years (for example, 1972, 1975), the profiles for men have changed dramatically, becoming much steeper and more peaked. According to the figures, the industry is now managed by a coterie of men 35–54 years old who command both high incomes and, presumably, high status. These are the employees who comprise the corporate management teams who have been brought in to run the complex organizations that now dominate the industry.

Indeed, remuneration at top management levels in the large department store chains, discount department store chains, and holding companies is on a par with that for executive officers in other industries. Ample evidence of this is contained in a *Forbes* report on the total compensation of the chief executive officers of the leading U.S. firms.[1]

		1978 Salary & Bonus ($)	1978 Total Remuneration ($)
Rapid American	Meshulam Riklis	729,000	770,000
Zayre	Maurice Segall	277,000	744,000
Dayton-Hudson	William A. Andres	490,000	733,000
Federated	Ralph Lazuras	450,000	630,000
Allied Stores	Thomas M. Macioce	500,000	604,000
Sears	Edward R. Telling	563,000	563,000
May Stores	David E. Babcock	350,000	557,000
J.C. Penney	Donald V. Seibert	374,000	471,000
K-Mart	Robert E. Dewar	435,000	453,000
F.W. Woolworth	Edward F. Gibbons	375,000	375,000

These compensation figures compare favorably with those of the largest, most affluent manufacturing firms among the Fortune 500. For the 802 companies surveyed by *Forbes*, total compensation averaged $306,000—significantly less than the tenth best-paid department store head. Below the highest-reaches of the corporate office are of course thousands of well-paid accountants, lawyers, chief buyers, advertisers, location specialists, personnel directors, systems analysts, and others. They are the workers, mostly men, in this industry who averaged $18,000 per year in 1975.

Their numbers have grown enormously with the transformation of the industry. From 67,000 supervisory workers throughout the sector in 1958, the ranks of the professional manager swelled to 117,000 by 1978.[2] In terms of full-time equivalent "census units," supervisors now put in nearly a third (31 percent) of the hours worked in the industry, up from 19 percent twenty years ago. Yet they remain a small percentage of the total labor force (6 percent) by actual count because these full-time workers are overshadowed in numbers by more than 1.7 million nonsupervisory workers, most on part-time schedules.

For women, though, the employment and earnings story is quite different. In fact, the trend in the age-earnings profiles is almost uncannily the exact reverse of that for white men (see Figure 6.2). In

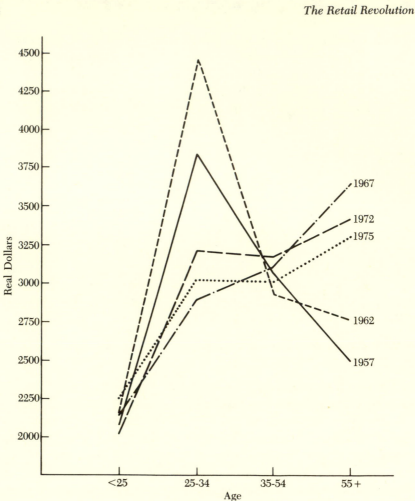

Figure 6.2. Age Earnings Profiles of White Women, 1957–1975 (real dollars, 1967 = 100). (*Source: LEED file analysis.*)

earlier years (for example, 1957 and 1962), women 25 to 35 years old used to earn considerably more than younger or older workers. This can probably be explained in terms of the hours worked by each group and the decline in skilled commission selling: Younger and older women were more prone to work part-time schedules while skilled "career saleswomen" worked full-time. But in more recent years the trend away from full-time sales jobs has flattened the profiles. There is, in some sense, no longer a return to longer job experience, for the limited skills one now needs on the job can be mastered in a matter of days or weeks rather than years. The traditional female sales occupations which required a knowledge of the

Table 6.5.   New England Department Store Industry Earnings (Current Dollars) Distribution for Full-Year Workers by Sex, 1975

	% < $3,000	% < $5,000	% > $15,000
Female	34.3	65.7	.3
Male	15.4	28.0	20.9

SOURCE: LEED file analysis.

products to be sold as well as certain promotional skills, have been "deskilled." What is more, the deskilling process—discussed at greater length later in this chapter—has actually led to a decline in real annual wages (except for older workers) as increases in hourly wages have been more than offset by decreases in average annual hours and by inflation.

The resulting disparity in earnings between men and women currently employed in the industry is highlighted in Table 6.5. While one-fifth of all men earn over $15,000 a year—most in management positions and in the few commission jobs left—*only three out of every one thousand women* are found in the same earnings category. Over a third earn less than $3,000 and almost two thirds earn less than $5,000 annually. Only four out of ten men in the industry earn so little. The conclusion one must inevitably draw is that the department store industry in its economic expansion has sorted itself out into a distinct dual economy—in this case a dual economy based partly on age but much more on sex.

The dual occupation and earnings structure in 1975 is vividly pictured in Figure 6.3. The modal income range for women is $2,000–$3,000 while that for men is found in the $12,000–$15,000 group. Again these numbers exclude seasonal workers, but include (especially among women and the low-income range of men) a majority of part-time employees. The dualism of 1975 is clearly more exaggerated than the occupation/earnings structure that existed in 1957 before the transformation of the industry had progressed to its current state (see Figure 6.4).

Despite the sharp polarity in annual earnings, a higher proportion of women rely on department store employers for their sole source of wage income. Two out of every five men in the industry have jobs outside the sector which pay more than their retailing jobs, and only 42 percent report department stores as their only source of earnings. In contrast, the department store job is the *sole* wage source for 56 percent of the women in the industry and the primary job for another 14 percent. Still, for only a tiny fraction of its labor force does the

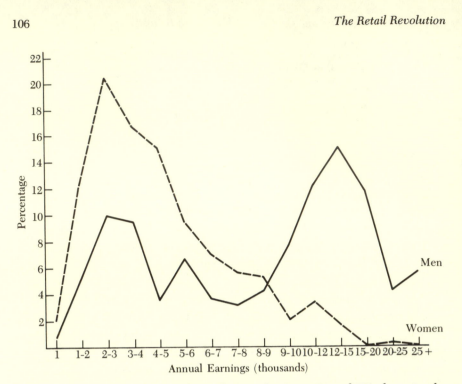

Figure 6.3. 1975 Earnings Distribution for Year-Round Workers in the New England Department Store Industry, by Sex. (*Source: LEED file analysis.*)

industry provide an ample source of family support. While retail trade can no longer be considered a poor relative of the manufacturing sector in terms of size or economic power, it is more than ever a provider of marginal employment opportunity for all but a small number of its workforce.

Minimum Wage Laws and Labor Costs in the Industry

Despite the low average wage in the industry, payroll costs constitute up to 50 percent of total department store expenses after the purchase of stock. According to an executive in one large store, "At one time the proportion was even higher and we had to automate and displace as many workers as possible in response to a cost squeeze." The chairman of the board of another store complained about minimum wages, repeating the often-heard charge that wage floors have hurt employment of young people in retail stores. "We have fewer jobs available," he said, "and if we have to pay we will settle for the older

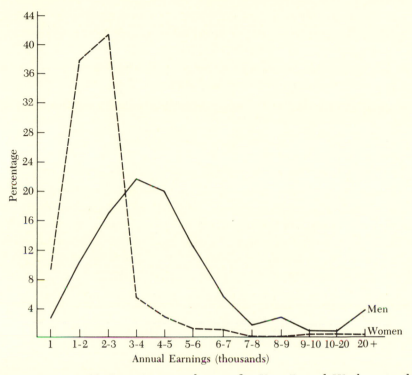

Figure 6.4. 1957 Earnings Distribution for Year-Round Workers in the New England Department Store Industry, by Sex. (*Source: LEED file analysis*.)

worker if the younger ones cost us beyond their worth. The minimum wage is absolutely detrimental."

Statistics generated from the LEED file do not support this contention. Although the national minimum wage increased four times between 1957 and 1974, rising from $1.00 to $2.00 an hour, the proportion of the department store labor force age 19 or less actually grew from 21.1 to 31.6 percent, while the proportion of nonwhite employment made up of youth expanded from 10 to 14.1 percent. One might have expected just the reverse if the minimum wage indeed presented a substantial disincentive to the hiring of youth.

A possible explanation of these findings was offered by a discount department store executive who noted that it is "hard to tell how much a minimum wage affects profits or employment because of the interrelationships involved in the 'eternal triangle' of sales, gross margins, and expenses. If the minimum wage did not exist, the ratio of payroll to sales would not have gone up as much, but in a competitive business, neither would have the gross margin." This suggests that since all employers pay the additional minimum wage, the cost is universally passed on to the consumer.

While labor costs are a large fraction of total expenses, it was noted in Chapter 2 that they comprise as little as 11 percent of total sales price in the discount sector and seldom more than 25 percent in the most exclusive specialty stores. Consequently, even if increases in the minimum wage affected every employee, and all increases were passed on to the consumer, the recent boost in the legal minimum from $2.65 to $2.90 an hour should have raised discount prices by no more than one percent. This is hardly sufficient, one would think, to make an employer suddenly substitute prime-age workers for the younger set he once hired in droves.

What needs to be explained is not the substitution of older for younger workers, but just the reverse. It is this which can be easily traced to the same deskilling process that underlies the observed flattening of female age-earnings profiles. With the ascendency of the low-margin discount chain, low-skilled "order-takers" and distribution workers could be substituted for more highly skilled salespersons and display designers. This transformation permitted the discounter to hire more than ever before from the teenage labor pool and to utilize a larger proportion of nonspecialized part-time workers. To compete, the traditional department store chains, as well as some stores within the holding company networks, altered production relations so as to draw from the same low-wage pool. It was consequently the fundamental change in production relations within the industry that ushered in the young worker as the typical employee of the modern retail firm.

A related institutional factor contributes to the rising demand for part-time workers. The expansion of employee fringe benefit packages in the industry may be much more important than the alleged need for flexible scheduling. The typical department store, whether unionized or not, offers a wide range of benefits: health insurance, pensions, merchandise discounts, holiday pay, paid vacation, life insurance, and various special bonuses. Together the value of these has rapidly increased as a percentage of total compensation. In most cases, however, these benefits are only available to full-time employees. The collective bargaining contract for one of the largest department stores, for example, stipulates paid Blue-Cross, Blue-Shield coverage only for workers who average twenty or more hours per week. Life insurance is not available to those employed less than forty weeks a year; retirement annuities are similarly available only to "full-time" workers.

As a consequence, department store employers, facing intense competition, have turned to part-time workers in order to cut their overall labor costs. The youth labor market naturally provides a ready supply of such workers. This type of cost pressure more than offsets the effect of a rise in minimum wages, making the latter pale in significance as a determinant of who is hired into the industry.

The Decline in Commission Selling

Measures intended to economize on labor cost have also been undertaken in the area of commission selling. With the movement toward "order-takers" and away from career salespersons, commissions on white goods have been reduced from 6–7 percent to 3–4 percent in some of the major chains. This marks the first stage in moving away from commission selling altogether. Today little merchandise is sold through the "upper tier" commission segment in the traditional department store and virtually none at all in the discount sector.

As a consequence, there are reduced earnings differentials in the sales divisions of major stores. In one Massachusetts division of a national holding company, commissioned salespeople now comprise less than 15 percent of the total sales force. Those still on commission average $24,000 a year compared with the average noncommission hourly wage of $4.75–$5.00/hour.

The loss of commission sales cannot be underestimated as a factor leading to the leveling of earnings profiles. The top commissioned salesperson in the shoe department of one store earned $54,000 in one year, excluding overtime. With his position phased out, the same job was handled by several relatively unskilled clerks at less than $5.00 per hour. There are obvious cost savings to the firm *if* the experience of the commission salesperson can be replaced by another merchandizing technique.

Since all modes of department stores, from cut-rate discount chains to Bloomingdale's, have adopted similar deskilled sales methods, it is not as surprising that there are no significant wage differences between modes. The typical cash register clerk with two years seniority in one of the more fashionable unionized Eastern department stores earned $3.75 per hour in 1978. The identical job paid $3.85 in the typical suburban discount chain. The differences in payroll/sales ratios between various retail modes is therefore a function of the number of people employed per sales dollar and the proportion of commission sales, not a function of hourly wage differentials.

Firms vary their labor costs not by adjusting the wage or the type of personnel they hire but by making conscious decisions over how many clerks will be available to service their customers. The goal of the manager is to find the optimal number that minimizes labor cost without discouraging shoppers from patronizing the store.

The Role of Unions

Only a small portion of the New England industry is unionized, with the majority of these workers in the Retail Clerks International and the Teamsters (warehouse workers). In early 1979 the Retail Clerks and the Amalgamated Meat Cutters merged to form the 1.2 million member United Food and Commercial Workers Union, affiliated with the AFL–CIO. The organization of the industry occurred soon after World War II, with the exception of a few independent company unions formed during the 1920's and 30's. Since the early organizing days, little union activity has taken place. "Not one nonunion operator has been actively organized in New England in thirty-five years," admitted one union official. Even the new suburban units of companies unionized long ago have remained unorganized. Where unionization has been successful, it has been due to spill-over from the more widely organized grocery store sector. Bradlee's is one hundred percent union as a result of being a division of the Stop & Shop Supermarket chain. Before terminating operations, J.M. Fields was fully unionized as a consequence of being owned by Food Fair.

The failure of unions to organize more widely in the industry is by no means entirely the result of lax organizing attempts. Given the high employee turnover in the sector plus the preponderance of part-time workers, organizing is much more difficult than in the traditional manufacturing sector or even the public sector. The age of the workforce is also a contributing factor to organizing problems.

Perhaps the greatest impediment to organizing is the very competitive nature of the industry. In its organizing drives the union is simply not in the position to offer promises of substantial wage or benefit increases. This will continue to be true until the industry as a whole can be organized, spreading the cost of wage and benefit improvements across all firms.

The result of union impotence and the competitive nature of the industry is that union and nonunion wages and fringe benefit packages are almost identical. The major difference between the union and nonunion sectors is reflected in the degree of latitude management has over the organization of production and over instituting productivity improvements. In the unionized sector these are the subject of collective bargaining, although management in the organized firms universally agree that the unions have not interfered with their attempts to "rationalize" production. As long as total membership is not eroded by lay-offs, firms are apparently able to introduce labor-saving equipment, reduce the workforce, and reorganize production without opposition from the union. Given the high turnover rate in the industry, attrition has been sufficient to accomplish this end. Management consistently points to the "good relations" they have with the union.

Regardless of their relationship, the Retail Clerks were able to make some progress in their 1979 round of negotiations with the major organized stores. Under the recently initiated contracts, hourly wages will be raised to a $4.80 minimum by 1981 when the national minimum wage goes to $3.35. Union representatives see this "as a real improvement," but argue that "it will take years to gain greater respectability for the union in the eyes of nonunionized workers."

Training

In the transition to a less-skilled labor force, many industry sources admit that in-house training programs have become "virtually nonexistent." The president of one large discount chain notes that his firm did not provide adequate training at the cash register level or at the local management level and that this was "one of the main weaknesses of the whole retail business."

According to the employee manual of a leading department store, a sales manager receives twelve weeks of on-the-job training. The first two weeks are spent in sales as a regular clerk, followed by eight weeks spent with an experienced sales manager, and finally two weeks of assisting a store buyer. A cash register clerk at the most prestigious establishment will receive two days of classroom training and off-floor instruction. The few exceptions to this rule are noteworthy.

Caldor, one of the fastest growing and most profitable of the New England discount chains, is known throughout the industry for its excellent training programs. The firm has its own "college of retail knowledge," which is in their built-in Executive Training Program.

Unlike most other chains, 80 percent of their store managers are developed from stock boys and clerks who began with the organization. Anyone from the outside must have a one year "apprenticeship" prior to full control as a store manager.

A universal complaint voiced by department store executives is that the hardest jobs to fill are those that are the lowest paid. The firms argue that there is a problem of discipline, but also admit that there is a lack of incentive to work at low-skill jobs, particularly those in the warehouse. In interviews, the chief executives of several firms charged that high welfare payments are a significant work disincentive affecting their ability to hire at the low end. Yet few firms take advantage of the CETA program to recruit workers, and there seems to be little movement in the industry toward more intensive training programs or voluntary wage increases as a means of attracting, as some industry officials put it, "a better class of workers."

There is a fundamental circularity in the industry's employment practices. Little training and low wages have led to the enormous turnover rates noted in the last chapter. Given the high turnover rate, however, there is little incentive for firms to offer training of a specific or general nature. The industry appears to have become inured to this development, perhaps preferring to put up with the turnover problem instead of making the changes that would be necessary to win a more stable workforce.

Productivity and Technology

The transformation in the modes of retail production which has brought about these enormous changes in the labor process rests on two factors: the revolutionary change in ownership patterns within the industry, and sweeping changes in technology. Historically, the two have gone hand-in-hand. The displacement of the small independent family-owned operation by large multi-unit corporate structures was fostered by the introduction of electronic data processing (EDP) and the expanded use of the print and electronic media in advertising. The holding company developed before these innovations and, because of its decentralized day-to-day operations, is less dependent on them. The large national and regional chains, however, are so dependent on EDP that it is not farfetched to assume that the technology itself helped to create many of them, just as the invention of the elevator allowed the building of skyscrapers. The computer provides economies of scale that yield a competitive edge over the alternative modes of production. Although computers are now found performing many aspects of retail work, their impact has been particularly significant in the area of inventory control.

The introduction of computerized inventory equipment in the mid-1960's enabled major retail chains to make sizable investments in labor-saving automation. The competitive pressure to maximize selling space productivity and minimize inventory investment (particularly in light of double-digit interest rates) has become so great that, according to industry sources, stores can no longer afford large stockrooms but instead must rely on regional distribution centers. Adding to this pressure are high freight costs, which have risen to the point where commercial shipping in the long-run costs more than establishing one's own distribution network. The coordination of this complex and centralized inventory strategy requires EDP investment.

Linked to a central computer, point-of-sale equipment is the sophisticated counterpart of the traditional cash register. This equipment provides instant detailed sales data, presumably reduces clerical errors, and provides on-line inventory controls. Additional benefits to the firm include rapid cash register balancing, reduced audit expense, and speeded credit authorization.

Retailers also argue that point-of-sale technology permits the merchandiser to respond more quickly to sales trends, thus avoiding out-of-stock situations which cost them sales, or overstocking which ties up capital funds. K-Mart uses the system to supplement the judgment of management in forecasting volume. This is particularly important in fast-changing fashion merchandising.

The chains have also added EDP controls directly in the warehouse. Computer-linked scanners are positioned to read information from cartons as they move on automated high-speed conveyor belts. Computer-prepared shipping lists and schedules serve as inventory control units to check container contents as merchandise is loaded and unloaded. These procedures have been lauded by the industry as methods for reducing the need to manually issue invoices and the need to manually correct punch cards for product identification and manifest preparation. Use of the system not only results in significant reductions in staff requirements but also is credited with decreasing inventory theft and accelerating merchandise flow. Additional computer-generated economies are obtained through more efficient scheduling of truck deliveries and a reduction in downtime due to the control and coordination of truck and automotive equipment maintenance. Each of these innovations has tended to reduce the amount of labor needed in the warehouse without increasing the skill level of the work.

The executive of one large regional discount department store chain summed up the importance of automation in the following way:

> *The more we grow, the more we realize that control is the name of the game. Now we tend to take the computer for granted. The fact is that without it we probably could not operate anywhere near as efficiently as we do.*

This is not to say, however, that automation has solved every problem. One executive at a major department store in Boston added a note of levity to the otherwise enthusiastic reception of the computerized store. When asked whether the new technology helped to reduce cost, he responded, "Yes and no. Data generation is expensive. We're spending a thousand times more on data, but we are not making a-thousand-times-better decisions."

The cost itself is a problem. Converting to electronic point-of-sale equipment is extremely expensive. One regional division of a large national holding company is presently spending $2 million to convert from mechanical to computerized cash registers in just three stores. Very few independents can afford this labor-saving technology. As a consequence their average payroll to sales ratio runs anywhere from 5 to 11 percentage points higher than the discount chains, and 4 to 10 points higher than the full-price chains. Competing in such a market has become a more tenuous proposition to a great extent because of the technology itself. In this sense the whirring and beeping of the computer has been the death knell of the traditional independent.

Beyond point-of-sale computerized equipment and the automated warehouse, department stores are finding other ways of cutting labor costs. Some chains are installing telephone equipment which allows one centralized switchboard to replace individual switchboards at branch stores. Others are eliminating their own fleets of delivery trucks and instead relying on United Parcel Service and Parcel Post. Increasingly, manufacturers are being coaxed to offer merchandise which is already pre-packaged and pre-priced. The department store dictates the price to the supplier and the supplier prints it as part of normal packaging, thus eliminating in-store marking and most display work. According to union officials, this practice has eliminated 2,000 marking jobs in the city of Detroit alone.

Other stores unabashedly admit to speed-up. One large discount chain, which was relatively unprofitable before a recent change in management, told us that the new executive team consciously let it be known that "we can only have 80 percent of the staff we had three years ago, so the remaining people must sell more." Supervisors were urged to press cash register employees to work more quickly and warehouse handlers to process more merchanidse in an eight hour day. Behind this was the not so subtle threat that the firm could follow the path of W.T. Grant, J.M. Fields, and numerous others if productivity did not improve.

Transportation, Advertising, and Productivity

In many ways the most significant technological advances affecting department stores, and their use of labor in particular, are not those endogenous to the industry. Rather they are the innovations in family transportation and mass media which have revolutionized housing patterns and advertising.

The growth of the suburban mall and discount strip and the demise of the downtown store are obviously a function of the exodus from the city permitted by the automobile. Land-intensive modes of retail production have replaced older multi-story department stores. Shopping has moved from downtown locations to bedroom suburbs. As a by-product, shopping occurring during evening hours has become a family event.

Changes in advertising techniques, however, have had an even more profound impact on the industry. The sheer amount of product promotion has expanded at a much more rapid pace than total personal commodity consumption, growing from $5.7 billion to $33.5 billion between 1950 and 1976 (see Table 6.6). At the same time there has been a shift toward larger amounts of television advertising at the expense of other media. In 1950 only 3 percent of all advertising expenditures accrued to television, while over a third went for news-

Table 6.6.   **Advertising and Personal Commodity Consumption Expenditures, 1950–1976 (billions of dollars)**

	1950	1960	1970	1976	% Increase 1950–1976
Personal Commodity Consumption	129	194	350	597	463
Advertising Expenditures	5.7	12.0	19.6	33.5	588

SOURCE: *Statistical Abstract of the United States, 1977*, p. 429 and p. 844.

Table 6.7.   Advertising Expenditures by Medium (Percentage Distribution)

	1950	1960	1970	1977
Newspapers	36.3	31.0	29.3	29.2
Radio	10.6	5.8	6.7	6.8
Television	3.0	13.3	18.3	20.1
Magazines	8.4	7.6	6.5	5.6
Direct Mail	14.1	15.3	14.1	14.0
Other	27.6	27.0	25.1	24.3
	100.0	100.0	100.0	100.0

SOURCE: *Statistical Abstract of the United States, 1978*, p. 855, table, 1489.

paper promotion. By 1977 television had absorbed over a fifth of all advertising, its growth being at the expense of newspapers, magazines, and radio (see Table 6.7).

The more than proportional growth in advertising and the increased dependence on television reflects an astoundingly radical change in the "production function" for retail services. It ultimately explains the "missing middle" in the labor force. Advertising has become a substitute for sales personnel, particularly the audio-video medium which is the closest substitute of all. Retailers have turned to the mass media to "sell" the customer, leaving the less-skilled clerical/cash register tasks to store employees. As a consequence, the skilled salespeople who knew fabrics and stitching, sizes, and wearability are fast disappearing from the department store. In their place the customer must now rely largely on television messages and brand-name recognition for information on such matters as product use and quality.

Having proven itself highly productive in the discount store, this deskilling of the labor force has generally permeated all retail modes with the possible exception of the higher-priced specialty store. It is no longer a futuristic fantasy to anticipate the day when families will order merchandise through a two-way cable TV installation in their own homes. One such system, offering groceries and products from the Sears catalogue, as well as airline schedules, news, and a bill-paying service, is now being tested in Coral Gables, Florida. A similar system has been operated by the British Post Office for about two years. The ultimate effect of this technology could be to eliminate the department store altogether, leaving only large warehouses and automated order-filling equipment. The effect on labor is almost incalculable.

Productivity and Employment

The sum total of all these technological and managerial innovations, combined with the shift from higher to lower payroll/sales ratio modes of production, has spurred advances in measured productivity and led to a relative decline in labor demand. This is nowhere more true than in New England which has traditionally been the first to exhibit new trends. Data from the *New England Census of Retail Trade* for 1963 through 1977 illustrate these changes.

Table 6.8 reveals aggregate sales, employment, and payroll trends in this region's department store industry. Figure 6.5 indicates that through 1972, real sales volume grew much more rapidly than employment. This is particularly true during the discount boom (1963–1967) when annual real sales per worker increased from $22,294 to $26,181, a 17.4 percent increase. During this period real sales grew by better than 50 percent, while firms expanded employment by only 28 percent to sell this added volume. On an output per person/hour basis, the measured advance in productivity during this period is even greater since the employment numbers fail to account for the growth in part-time employment. Using national average weekly hours data and assuming no change in days worked per year, output per person/hour grew by 22.8 percent between 1963 and 1967, or better than 4 percent per year.

Despite this increase, the payroll-to-sales ratio rose until 1972, partly as a result of superimposing a highly paid corporate structure on top of the existing industry, and partly as a result of rising real wages for all workers during this period of aggregate economic expansion. The real productivity increase, therefore, did not necessarily result in higher profits.

In the following five-year-period ending in 1972, real sales continued to expand but at a slower pace (+29.5%), while employment

Table 6.8.   Aggregate Sales, Employment, and Payroll in New England Department Stores, 1963–1977 (Sales & Payroll in Thousands of Dollars)

	Sales (Current $)	Sales (1967 = 100)	Employment	Payroll (Current $)	Payroll/Sales Ratio
1963	1,206,546	1,272,728	57,088	164,856	.1366
1967	1,919,481	1,919,481	73,317	269,358	.1403
1972	2,967,643	2,485,463	88,272	411,994	.1388
1977	3,893,936	2,358,532	82,680	518,313	.1331

SOURCE: U.S. Bureau of the Census, *Census of Retail Trade*, 1963–1977.

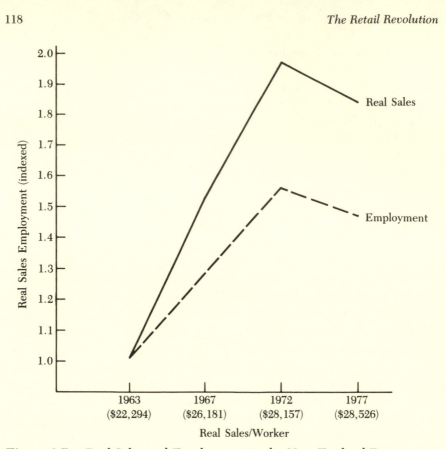

Figure 6.5. Real Sales and Employment in the New England Department Store Industry, 1963–1977 (1963 = 1.00). (*Source: Bureau of the Census, U.S. Department of Commerce*, Census of Retail Trade, *1963–1977*.)

grew by 20 percent. The result was a 7.6 percent increase in the real-sales-per-worker ratio. This corresponds to the initial period of market saturation that followed the discount boom. Most of the growth in productivity can be attributed to the shake-out of high-cost firms and the adaptation of new technology.

The most recent period saw an actual decline in real sales, particularly as a consequence of the 1975 recession and its aftermath. The 5.1 percent decline in sales was matched by a 6.3 percent reduction in employment so that productivity was roughly constant, rising no more than .3 percent per year. Presumably the inability to curtail employment further is tied to the growth in the managerial workforce incorporated in the new industry structure.

During the overall period from 1963 to 1977, real productivity grew by 28 percent and the industry was able to reduce its payroll/sales ratio by 5 percent, from .1403 (in 1967) to .1331. Whether the industry can continue to boost productivity during the next decade will primarily be a function of its ability to make additional cost savings through technology. At least for the present the transformation in modes seems to have reached a plateau, so that productivity advances like those that took place between 1963 and 1967 cannot be expected. Yet, given the fact that labor still comprises nearly half of all department store costs, there is still profit to be made in deskilling and displacing the labor force. The logic of this does not escape the chief executive officers in the industry. As one of them candidly admitted, "I spend half my waking hours trying to figure out ways to become less dependent on labor."

In the recession of 1980, the *Wall Street Journal* reports, firms like F.W. Woolworth, Dayton-Hudson, and K-Mart are trying to cut costs and boost productivity by reducing sales forces, curtailing travel by executives and merchandise buyers, and postponing capital spending. Many executives reluctantly have given up their personal secretaries for the services of a secretarial pool and economical word-processing machines. In the 1980's, says the chief executive of one of the largest holding companies, "the whole subject of productivity is a very, very major one." How much it can be boosted by these types of economies is still to be seen. But what seems sure is that there is no reversing the trends in the labor process that began with the discount store and the advertising blitz and now seems to be on the verge of entering the head office.

Endnotes

1. *Forbes Magazine*, "How Much Does the Boss Make?" Volume 123, No. 12 (June 11, 1979).
2. U.S. Department of Labor, Bureau of Labor Statistics, *Employment and Earnings Statistics for the U.S., 1909–1978*.

Selected Sources

Blumenthal, Ralph, "Legal Problems for Discounters," *The New York Times* (February 2, 1979), p. D1.

Duncan, Delbert I., and Stanley C. Hollander, *Modern Retailing Management: Basic Concepts and Practices*, 9th ed. (Homewood, Illinois: Richard D. Irwin, 1977).

Streeter, Bill, "White House Eyeing Robinson-Patman Act: Repeal Is Possible," *Industrial Distribution* (November 1975), p. 41.

Tarpey, Lawrence X. Sr., "Buyer Liability Under Robinson-Patman Act," *Journal of Marketing*, Vol. 36 (January 1972), p. 38.

"Will Congress End Fair Trade?" *Business Week* (February 17, 1975), p. 82.

Chapter 7

THE ROLE OF GOVERNMENT

The impact of government policy on industries such as hospitals and aerospace is readily apparent, but the extent to which government has influenced the restructuring of the retail sector is often not fully appreciated. Economic and demographic trends are not solely responsible for the transition in retail mode dominance or the changes in investment and ownership patterns described in this volume. Government legislation, at both the federal and state levels, has provided a major impetus to this transformation.

The Robinson-Patman Act and Resale Price Maintenance legislation (fair trade laws) have had perhaps the greatest impact on the restructuring of the retail industry. These laws were passed during the thirties, after the Great Depression, when there was a general wave of legislation limiting chain-store growth. Designed to limit price cutting, the intention of this legislation was to ensure small retailers a continuing place in the market. A number of consequences resulting from their passage ultimately led to the repeal of state fair trade laws during the 1960's and 1970's. Federal legislation over-rode all remaining such laws in 1976. The Robinson-Patman Act is still in effect today, but it is the hope of many retailers and government officials that the Act will soon be revised.

Robinson-Patman
Price Discrimination Act of 1936

Sometimes referred to as the "anti–A & P law," the Robinson-Patman Act was drafted with the intent of eliminating unfair price concessions that large firms enjoyed and equalizing prices charged by manufacturers for goods purchased directly and indirectly by buyers.

Under the provisions of the Act, a vendor involved in interstate trade may not give a lower price to one buyer than another under the following circumstances:

1. If the buyers take commodities of the same grade or quality.
2. If the price difference:
   (a) substantially lessens competition;
   (b) tends to create a monopoly;
   (c) injures, destroys, or prevents competition with vendor or buyer, or customers of either.
3. If the price difference is not merely for the purpose of "due allowance for differences in the cost of manufacture, sale, or delivery resulting from the differing methods or quanitites in which such commodities are to purchasers sold or delivered," or one offered "in good faith to meet the equally low price of a competitor."[1]

The Act neither requires nor prevents the use of discounts of any kind; it simply places limits on the use of them. It does not apply directly to the retail prices stores charge, but to the wholesale prices retailers and other organizations are charged for goods and certain services rendered in conjunction with their purchases. Ironically, only one section of the Act is directed exclusively at buyers, despite the law's intent to limit the buying power of large chains. The majority of the Act is directed at restricting the power of manufacturers and wholesalers. As with the history of other anti-trust measures, the actual impact of the legislation has often been directly contrary to its original intent.

To comprehend the paradoxical effect of the Robinson-Patman Act one must first understand the different buying practices of small and large firms. Centralized buying, characteristic of large chain store operations and holding companies, places a large part of the authority over buying merchandise outside the individual store. Merchandise buyers, located in the central office, are given the responsibility for purchasing from manufacturers and wholesalers, while individual store managers are restricted to simply retailing the merchandise. Some corporate executives, however, have become aware that individual branch stores will be less profitable if their store managers are merely puppets of the home office. For this reason, they often allow individual store managers to select much of their merchandise from lists supplied by the central office. A few holding companies allow store buyers the liberty to refuse goods selected by central buyers, but this is generally the extent of such freedom. The reason for this is that the benefits of central buying are extensive and include (1) the elimination of brokerage fees and (2) the availability of "quantity-discounts" proportionate to the size of the order.

Decentralized buying, on the other hand, is characteristic of smaller firms where the size of individual orders is generally much smaller. As a consequence, the independent is often forced to depend on a broker when ordering and cannot take advantage of quantity discounts. There are, however, benefits of decentralized buying, including (1) the ability to accommodate the specific tasks of the local customer and (2) less duplication of decision-making tasks by central and local management.

Still, the use of a broker, or "indirect" buying, entails an added expense for both the wholesale buyer and seller of merchandise since the brokerage fee is often shared. Centralized buying is therefore attractive to both the manufacturer and large retailer because it avoids this cost.

According to the Robinson-Patman Act, vendors who use brokers for *part* of their sales may not grant lower prices to reflect the nonpayment of brokerage fees on any direct sales. This was originally designed to benefit the smaller firm that must operate through a broker, but it has come to have just the opposite effect.

A loophole in the Act allows vendors who sell *all* their output directly to retailers to grant lower prices than they might ask if using a broker. This provision discourages some manufacturers from indirect selling to small firms, since to do so would restrict their ability to offer discounts to their large-volume customers. This severely limits the access smaller retailers have to popular brand-name merchandise.

Figure 7.1 illustrates this point. The manufacturer who sells both indirectly and directly must include what is essentially a surcharge on the price paid by the direct buyer. If this were not required under the Robinson-Patman Act, the manufacturer could charge a lower price to the direct retailer and presumably increase the sales volume of its product. Where the brokerage fee is a significant cost, it often benefits the manufacturer to discontinue his indirect business to capture more of the direct trade.

While brokerage fees are explicitly covered under the Robinson-Patman Act, quantity discounts (reductions in the price granted according to the amount purchased at a given time, or to the total purchase made within a specified time period) are not mentioned in the legislation and are therefore legal. Because the size of a discount is based on the quantity of merchandise bought, the exclusion tends

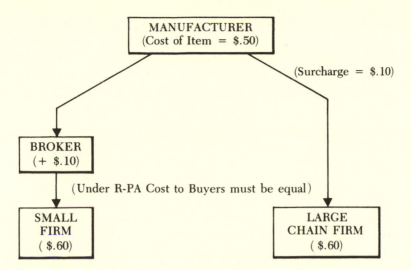

Figure 7.1. Cost to Buyer under Indirect and Direct Selling.

to strongly favor large chain stores. As one management expert stated:[2]

> To the layman it would seem that suppliers would have to justify quantity discounts on the basis of "cost of manufacture, sale, or delivery." But the Federal Trade Commission and the courts have not taken this position; instead, they have ruled that wholesale trade discounts result in no injury to competition and therefore constitute no violation of the Act.

Under the Robinson-Patman Act, other types of discounts must be offered uniformly within each "trade group," and trade groupings recognized by a supplier must have a factual basis. Because trade groupings (retail modes) are neither mutually exclusive nor clearly defined by law, it is legally difficult to determine the existence of injury to competition by reason of differential discounts. Under the R–PA, a supplier may offer discounts "as long as the same proportionate reduction is given to all competing comparable buyers." But the legislation does not define terms such as "proportionate" and "comparable," so that unfair advantage may still accrue to certain firms. This is particularly a problem in saturated markets where one store's loss is another's gain.

The Robinson-Patman Act was also intended to equalize the treatment and services available to all modes of retailing in the areas of product promotion and advertising. According to the law, "co-op" or "support" money for advertising provided by manufacturers to retailers should be equally available. However, only the larger retailers have the funds to support their end of advertising campaigns and therefore smaller firms are excluded from this "subsidy." One independent who cannot afford to engage in co-op television advertising explained:

> *You really have to be big to get the co-op money. We aren't receiving any of it partly because we don't go after it. Large stores are entitled to it because they can buy more. It's all relative. Resource salesmen seek out large stores like Jordan March to advertise merchandise. Even if we get 50 percent of the money, larger stores can get 75 percent to 80 percent whether its against the law or not. They have the buying power. This is where smaller stores can use a little more ingenuity by possibly grouping together. But the Robinson-Patman Act should not have been written.*

In 1960 there were 130 R–PA complaints and 45 cease-and-desist orders. In 1974 there were only two complaints and seven orders. Apparently a lot of treble damage cases involving the Act are now handled privately and settled out of court. In 1966 revision of the R–PA was recommended by the National Commission on Marketing and in 1975 a revision or possible repeal of the law was recommended by the Ford Administration. But the law still stands.

Critics of the Act state that its provisions interfere with efficient methods of wholesaling and retailing by allowing inefficient companies to survive. They also argue that the R–PA is inflationary because it maintains artificially high prices.

In contrast, and despite its weaknesses, independents are fighting to keep the Act. The National Small Business Association (NSBA), in conjunction with some 25 other national associations, has begun preparing a massive campaign against repeal efforts. The NSBA maintains that repeal would leave independents vulnerable to flagrant price discrimination and that some protection is better than none. NSBA's goal is greater public enforcement of the law by the Federal Trade Commission. Revision is seen as necessary; repeal is not. The battle shapes up to be a classic one between a slew of Davids and a few Goliaths.

Fair Trade Laws: Resale Price Maintenance

Fair trade laws (technically Resale Price Maintenance statutes) were legal mechanisms that permitted manufacturing firms to set a minimum on the price that retailers (and wholesalers) could charge for the products they produced. These laws gave manufacturers the power to require retailers to sell a manufacturer's brand-name of trade-marked products at a fixed price. Furthermore, most of the fair trade statutes authorized by individual states included a "nonsigner" provision, making it possible for manufacturers to easily operate fixed-price programs by allowing a contract with just one retailer to effectively bind all other retailers in the state.

Passed during the Depression, when small retailers were going out of business in large numbers as a result of low profit margins, legalized price-fixing was allowed to permit smaller stores a profit margin that larger retailers could not undercut. When discount department stores entered the industry, fair trade laws were used by full-price stores to attack discounters' low price competitive advantage.

The percentage of retail merchandise sold subject to Resale Price Maintenance fluctuated between 10 percent in the late 1930's and 1940's and 4 percent in the early 1970's. But this small percentage was concentrated among a limited range of consumer goods, so that it effectively precluded discounters from carrying certain product lines, including small consumer durables. In 1975 opponents of the law, backed by U.S. Senator Edward Brooke (R–Mass.), led a national attack on the last vestiges of the legislation. They claimed that the fair trade laws were inflationary, and estimated that such legislation cost consumers approximately $2 billion annually by increasing prices on fair trade goods by 18 to 27 percent. They cited examples including a set of golf clubs that listed for $220 in fair-trade areas, available in free trade areas for $136, and a stereo costing $1,390 in fair trade areas which sold for $950 where no such law existed.[3] By the end of the year, their lobbying effort proved successful and national anti-fair trade law legislation virtually eliminated this legal mechanism. By this time, however, many individual states had already relaxed their statutes.

Discount retailers led the fight against fair trade legislation and particularly the nonsigner clause well before Brooke began his effort. Opponents claimed that fair trade laws were unconstitutional, inflationary, and that their provisions were in direct conflict with a free-market economy. These arguments were influential in reducing the number of states with such laws from 45 in 1941 to 13 by 1975.

Fighting a losing battle, many manufacturers who defended the legislation argued that repeal would actually result in higher prices for the consumer. William Day, director of consumer relations and product sales at Westinghouse, told *Business Week* his company only fair-traded in the New York metropolitan area and then only because of the proliferation of dealers there.[4]

We are not completely overboard on fair trade, but it is beneficial to the consumer and the dealer in the New York area. If Fair Trade was eliminated there, the dealers would then lose control of their pricing and eventually would stop carrying certain items. This would reduce the number of places where an item is available and the price would rise.

While the actual repeal of nonsigner clauses and the laws themselves did not occur in New England states until the early 1970's, industry sources in the region indicate that the laws have generally been unenforced since the mid-1960's. This permitted the regional discount boom in the late 1960's and early 1970's. Many small merchants selling brand-name goods in fair-trade states came to realize that fair trade laws were not effectively protecting their market share. Large retailers were able to escape price-maintenance regulations by selling private-label products such as Sear's Kenmore line produced by Whirlpool. The proliferation of private labels reduced the efficacy of fair trade laws to the point where active support almost disappeared.

The repeal of fair trade laws may not have had a significant effect on the average price of merchandise but it had a profound effect on the department store industry as a whole. Repeal precipitated a virtually total restructuring of the retail sector.

Abolishing fair trade laws allowed discounters access to national brand-name merchandise that the conventional department store had traditionally monopolized. Discounters were then able to sell identical brand-name merchandise for lower prices. Traditional department stores, with their higher overhead, were simply unable to compete. Because of this, department stores were forced to eliminate basic low margin convenience items such as nonprescription drugs, as well as bulk commodities, including house paint and garden products, that they had traditionally carried. Today this merchandise is almost exclusively sold by discounters and specialty shops such as hardware stores and drug stores.

As a result of shifting merchandise lines, department stores were left with vacant floor space which forced them to discover new avenues of merchandise in order to maintain their market share. One strategy developed by department stores was to upgrade merchandise quality, catering to the fashion oriented customer. Department stores incorporated the specialty store concept within their walls through internal expansion and by concentrating mainly on decorative home furnishings and fashion apparel.

The shift involved more than substituting one line of merchandise for another. It made necessary new location strategies, extensive advertising campaigns, and an alteration in the image that department stores projected to targeted customer groups. Retailers relied heavily upon the management expertise and uniqueness of specialty stores as an essential element in easing the transition. As the president of a regional department store stated:

> *I have to admit, I feared the repeal of the fair trade laws, believing that discounters would "steal" certain lines of merchandise, which they did. Now I think it was the right thing to do. Department stores have had to learn to adapt and combat the price advantage and appeal of discounters by improving management, the atmosphere of the store, and the services available to the customer. In a way it added a new excitement to retail. With the right concept or formula, even though the price is cheaper elsewhere, customers will be attracted and they will spend their money where their needs are met. Department stores have learned that they do not need to be propped up by something artificial like fair trade laws.*

After losing market share to the discount sector all through the late 1950's and early 1960's, the full-price department store chains and holding companies have been able to stabilize their share, apparently through innovative merchandising. They retained 9 percent of the total General Merchandise Market, while discounters leveled off at between 11 and 13 percent (recall Table 2.1).

The repeal of the fair trade laws resulted in another major change in the department store industry. Because department stores no longer had government protection against the competitive price advantage of the discounters, the repeal gave further impetus to the knitting together of retail production modes through the ownership and acquisition of stores. Department store chains and holding companies were cognizant of the risk of narrowing their customer base too severely by specializing and trading-up at a time when inflation was driving even the wealthy to seek out bargains. Consequently, they began to establish bargain basements and increase their holdings of discount specialty stores.

The specialty store concept has also been successfully applied by discounters. Through the acquisition of lower-price specialty chains, discounters have broadened their customer base to include those who desire quality merchandise but cannot afford the accompanying high prices.

The repeal of the fair trade laws has forced dominant firms within each mode of the department store industry to develop new strategies in order to preserve and increase market share. Other firms within competing modes imitate these innovative strategies and adapt them to their own concepts. This action-reaction cycle narrows the distinctions between the modes and results in a further comingling of ownership. The application of new strategies has therefore resulted in a virtual revolution in the department store industry and has intensified the competitive struggle within modes as well as between them.

Recent Legislation

Recent legislation affecting the buying and selling practices of retailing and manufacturing firms appears to conflict with previous rulings over price-fixing in a free market. A little-publicized 1977 Supreme Court decision ruled that a manufacturer could limit the number and location of franchised sales outlets if such restrictions enhanced the producer's ability to compete in a wider market. Independent retailers are likely to be more severely affected by this ruling than large discount chains because brand-name manufacturers often have an interest in restricting sales to large-volume outlets which can quickly market excess inventory and enhance a product's image. This type of market restriction has now been held constitutional.

While actual price-fixing remains illegal, the 1977 decision gave manufacturers considerably more control over the distribution of their products and, in effect, allowed them to discourage vendors from doing business with some discounters. Manufacturers, however, argue that the 1977 decision broadens inter-brand competition, protects their franchised dealers, and upgrades the image of their products. By restricting the number and sites of their authorized dealers and closing accounts with those who sell to discounters, manufacturers are able to maintain higher prices.

One example of the response to the 1977 ruling involves Lanvin, a manufacturer of perfumes. After the court decision, Lanvin underwent a change of ownership and subsequently shut down for three months, cancelling all of its dealer arrangements. Upon reopening, Lanvin eliminated four-fifths of its previous outlets and raised its prices significantly.[5]

The ambiguities inherent within this 1977 Supreme Court decision are evident in the contradictory outcomes of later legal cases. For example, the Eastern Scientific Company of Providence, Rhode Island, contended that it had been cut off by a Swiss manufacturer's distributor for selling at a discount outside its assigned territory. A federal appeals court ruled that a resale price restriction, in effect price-fixing, was a legal part of territorial sale restrictions. Ironically in an earlier lawsuit, *Sony v. Horst A. Eiberger of Atlanta*, a federal court reached a diametrically opposed conclusion. In its findings the court concluded, "Sony's territorial restrictions had stifled intra-brand competition far more than they might have stimulated competition between brands." Sony was ordered to pay damages to one of its dealers of $153,416.[6] Needless to say, the ruling requires clarification if its principles are to be fairly and uniformly applied. While it is too early to accurately access the final impact of these court decisions, the bias inherent in these quasi-fair trade rulings favor the full price store chains and holding companies at the expense of discount chains. The tide, fostered by legislation, that began shifting in the late 1950's toward the discounter may be turning back toward the traditional store on the basis of court action. Even the most subtle moves of government affect this industry profoundly.

Blue Laws

Another example of government intervention are "Blue Laws," which prohibit the opening of certain retail establishments on Sunday. Reflecting the Christian heritage of the nation, these laws were originally designed to institutionalize the religious ideal that people should not work on the Sabbath. More recently, Blue Laws have been championed as a means of protecting the rights of workers in retail trade.

Since their inception, Sunday closing-laws have repeatedly been challenged and modified to more effectively serve the requirements of individual states. For example, the Blue Laws of New Hampshire are less stringent than those of Massachusetts because of the differing economies of the two states. A large percentage of New Hampshire workers are still employed in mill-based industry which operates six days a week. In order to accomodate the limited shopping time of these workers, it has been necessary through revisions in the law to permit the extension of store hours to include Sunday. The revision of Blue Laws has also occurred in many other New England states in response to consumer demand for extended shopping hours during the Christmas holiday season.

In Massachusetts, the provisions of state Blue Laws tend to favor smaller stores. According to the law, proprietor-run stores—"ma and pa" shops—are permitted to remain open on Sunday with no more than two employees in the store. This provision excludes larger would-be competitors from opening on Sunday and increases the volume of Sunday sales for small merchants. Firms owning large stores have been lobbying for a revision of state Blue Laws which would permit them to open on Sunday as well. Nonetheless there are some large retailers who oppose such a revision because the expense involved in paying employees time and a half for working on Sunday would be detrimental to their cost-containment strategies.

There are a number of other arguments cited in opposition to a revision in state Blue Laws. The most prevalent one is that repeal would ultimately kill small business. However, in defense of repeal, a representative of one discount department store chain in Massachusetts claimed that, although their stores are already open 72 hours a week, smaller stores in the area have not found it necessary to keep similar store hours in order to remain in business. Discount operators also defend repeal by arguing that it is the role of the small store to offer personal service and the role of the discount department store to offer the convenience of extended hours. They claim the law is preventing them from doing this job.

Another opposing argument often cited by union officials and retail employees is that retailers should not have the right to require full-time employees to work on Sunday. In response to this, retailers explain that the majority of their labor force is part-time (75 percent in New England); therefore requiring employees to work on Sunday would not be detrimental to their well-being or private lives. This may be true for some part-time workers, but many others also hold second jobs or attend school. A viable compromise would be to permit department stores to open on Sunday with the stipulation that employees be allowed to refuse to work on Sunday or be given more freedom in designing their own work schedules.

One argument cited in favor of the revision of Blue Laws is that as they stand today they discriminate against the growing number of women workers who are the primary shoppers for their families. Retailers claim that Blue Laws deny consumers the convenience of extended shopping hours.

Discounters and department stores have attempted to circumvent Blue Law regulations for many years. Searching for loopholes, retailers have gone to great lengths to sell merchandise on Sunday. An amusing example is Weston's Shoppers Center in Albany, New York, which utilized a "souvenir ploy" to sell merchandise on Sunday. In 1972 Weston's challenged New York state Blue Laws in court, contending that it was impossible to determine which merchandise could legally be sold on the Sabbath. The case was overturned by the New York State Court of Appeals, with the ruling that "reasonable men" could interpret the law and understand which items could legally be sold. After this ruling Weston's discovered a loophole in the law which permitted the Sunday sale of souvenirs. Weston's soon began opening on Sunday with large signs prominently displayed to warn customers that only "souvenirs" could be purchased. Because the state statute does not define "souvenir," it was possible to let consumers determine the meaning for themselves. The managers explained their position: "We tell the customers the law presumes that a reasonable man is able to determine in his own mind what a souvenir is. If a guy wants to buy an oil filter as a souvenir, we're not going to argue with him." The vagueness of the law continues to allow "reasonable men" to take advantage of this lack of definition.

The Paradox of Government Policy

It is apparent then that the Robinson-Patman Act and fair trade laws, no matter what their original intent, have not ensured the small retailer a place in the market. Limiting the pricing freedom of larger firms seemed to be the correct approach to such an objective, but in practice these laws provide further cost-cutting benefits for large retail companies by failing to regulate quantity discounts.

The provisions of the Robinson-Patman Act have encouraged retail management structures to grow in size and complexity. Corporate managers have fostered the development of centralized buying practices, and, despite the Robinson-Patman Act, firms are not prevented from using the weight of their large orders to discourage suppliers from doing business with smaller competitors. A firm's ability merely to place large-volume orders results in savings through the nonregulated allowance of quantity discounts.

The repeal of fair trade laws provided a major impetus to the restructuring of the department store industry, but again the change was, if anything, anti-small business. The repeal required firms to devise new competitive strategies which resulted in the merging of retail modes. Existing large firms reacted by forming retail conglomerates and moving into the discount sector. Repeal may therefore have been pro-consumer, but it can hardly be considered successful in fostering reduced concentration in the market. Whether this is simply a case of the "best laid plans of mice and men" or an example of the political clout of "big business" is hard to decipher. In either case, government policy has contributed mightily to the reorganization of retail trade and bears substantial responsibility for determining which modes prosper and which wane.

Endnotes

1. Delbert I. Duncan and Stanley C. Hollander, *Modern Retailing Management: Basic Concepts and Practices*, 9th ed. (Homewood, Illinois: Richard D. Irwin, 1977), p. 329.
2. *Ibid.*, p. 332.
3. "Will Congress End Fair Trade?" *Business Week* (February 17, 1975) p. 82.
4. *Ibid*, p. 83.
5. Ralph Blumenthal, "Legal Problems for Discounters ", *The New York Times*, (February 2, 1979), p. D1.
6. *Ibid*, p. D2.

Selected Sources

"Big Oil's Move into Retailing," *Chain Store Age Executive* (September 1976), p. 29.
"Federated Department Stores" (Boston: Harvard Business School Intercollegiate Case Clearing House, No. 375-147).
"Federated . . . and the Consumer Comeback," *Dun's Review* (December 1967), p. 38.
Slom, Stanley H., "Grant Testimony Shows It Lacked Curbs on Budget, Credit and Had Internal Woes," *The Wall Street Journal* (February 4, 1977).

Chapter 8

THE ROLE OF MANAGEMENT

While government legislation is instrumental in determining which modes of retail trade prevail, industry sources stress the importance of "good management" to the success of individual establishments. Good management is difficult to define and virtually impossible to measure, but to most retailers it is considered crucial in the struggle for survival.

By itself, this intangible factor cannot assure the success of retail trade where demographic or economic factors do not provide the proper environment. Yet one case study after another suggests that without good management, even an extraordinary market opportunity can turn sour. The narrow profit/sales margins in the industry, tied to intense market competition, require managers to be constantly vigilant or face the consequences. A litany of stories tell of how even billion-dollar retail giants have slipped into oblivion as the result of managerial error.

Sound financial reckoning, far-sighted location planning, and innovative marketing are all part of a good management strategy, but it is the human element that most retailers prefer to emphasize. "You have to understand," says the chairman of Federated's finance committee, "that retailing is not a capital-intensive business. The important types of planning are people planning and market planning, not capital planning."[1] Moreover, management at the local-store level can be as critical to a firm's success as the executives in the head office. "[The local manager] is where it really happens for Kresge," says one K-Mart competitor in Detroit, "and where it goes wrong for most other discounters. Among all of us who are playing 'catch up with Kresge,' store management is one area in the greatest need of improvement."[2]

The Management Factor

There is serious debate over what makes a good manager. Adaptability, leadership, and the ability to listen and observe are named most often as the premier qualities of an exceptional manager. Federated Department Stores, frequently cited as a paragon of management, is described by a former vice president as having "progressive and effective management in which there is a willingness to experiment [and] a tough standard of achievement."[3] Harold Krensky, Federated's current president, claims:[4]

> *Every president or top executive has his own style but I believe that the basic task of all managers is the same—to motivate people to get the highest return. People often talk of Mr. Fred's [Fred Lazarus, Jr., former president of Federated] 'on the wall' technique as his major management tool, but above all he was a tremendous motivator of people.*

Motivation, then, seems to be the key. Every six months, "Mr. Fred," a legendary leader in the industry, would meet with division heads at Federated and post the expense performance of the top divisions "on the wall," challenging the other divisions to compete. His tough standard of achievement allegedly was successful in spurring division heads to keep costs in line, making Federated for a long time the most profitable of the full-price department store chains.

A *Harvard Business Review* article written by three management consultants stresses another factor, flexibility, as the key element in retail survival. This requirement is particularly needed in a fast-changing industry![5]

> *For retail executives, the shortening life cycle [of retail businesses] puts a premium on being able to adapt to changing trends and to work with new management ideas. To cope with continual change, retailers must consider the use of different management styles or even different management groups during succeeding stages of development.*

The competitiveness of the department store industry and the speed with which fashion and consumer tastes change suggest that the ability to survive in the market depends on the ability to pick up cues which originate on a local level, identify new trends, and adapt. This requires, according to industry experts, managerial responsiveness to lower-level employees. It is the local store manager who is in the closest proximity to the consumer and can best observe the success or failure of specific merchandising strategies.

Thus, one important difference among department stores is the extent to which management decisions are centralized—that is, made from the "top down." While many firms stress uniformity among divisions and strong control by central management, two of the most successful firms in the department store industry, Federated and K-Mart, are known for the autonomy they allow branch managers. Local managers with both companies are generally better-trained, better-paid than managers in the industry as a whole, and their ideas for policy development or revision are considered to be more highly valued.

Decentralization has occured naturally for Federated because of the way in which the company originated. Each Federated division, with the exception of the new discount chains, began as a successful, locally managed independent with its own well-established identity. It is in this sense that Federated has been described as an association of entrepreneurs, "a group of proudly individualistic enterprises contained within a strong corporate unity."[6] Ralph Lazarus, Federated's Chairman, describes the company as an "upside down organization," with buyers and sales staff at the top of the organizational chart and the chairman at the bottom, forming an upside-down pyramid. "Everyone below this line, including me," he says, drawing a line which separates the local buyers from the Divisional Merchandise Managers "below" them, "exists only to add to the growth and profitability of these units. We are all here only as long as we help these guys to be more effective."[7]

Federated has worked to put responsibility for buying, management, and profit as far down the hierarchy and as close to the consumer as possible, avoiding for example, a central buying staff. Although local buying sacrifices certain economies of scale which other firms have been able to use to their advantage, Federated has built its success on the premise that each store and each community is different and that it pays to treat them accordingly.

This has also proven successful in the discount mode regardless of the apparently uniform appearance of each outlet. At K-Mart, store managers are given more independence than most discount store managers. Although buying and setting retail ceiling prices is done centrally, local managers can determine the selection and amount of merchandise, lower the prices set by corporate marketing staff, and have a say in how advertising money is spent in their area. Longer training periods and a comparatively high salary (in the $25,000–$30,000 range) accompany this greater responsibility. To build this kind of staff, K-Mart's local management is trained on the inside. No one can become a store manager who has not spent at least ten years with the company.

Good managers in all industries have certain administrative abilities in common, but executives both inside and outside retailing suggest that within the industry there are management problems which require special expertise. One of these involves expansion and acquisition decisions. Knowing how to use expertise in one retail line to expand into another requires careful planning. When Zayre, for example, added yet another specialty chain store to its operations, a company official explained the reasons behind this particular expansion.[8]

> *T. J. Maxx draws upon our background in soft goods and employs many of the merchandising techniques that have proven successful in our Hit or Miss shops, but applies them to a broader range of categories, including men's, women's, boy's, girl's, and infant's.*

Zayre apparently recognized the significant advantages and managerial economies involved in building on a past success rather than attempting an entirely new merchandising style.

In contrast, Mobil Oil's acquisition of Montgomery Ward came out of a desire to diversify its operations. The oil company's management, however, recognized that the very fact of diversification meant special organizational problems. Mobil's vice-president for planning told *Chain Store Age:*[9]

> *When our diversification quest finally led us to Wards, we told our board and management committee that we weren't deep enough to divert our energies to another business. We weren't broad-based in our management skills, so any acquisition had to have good management.*

Rawleigh Warner, Jr., Mobil's chief, added "I don't see an operating role for Mobil in Wards for one fundamental reason. We're not retailers, and we learned long ago that you can't appoint someone and expect him to do an effective job in a business that he doesn't know."[10] Montgomery Ward's management has been given free reign over day-to-day operations, while Mobil's board ultimately controls long-run investment strategy.

Considerations of expertise put some constraints on mergers and buy-outs of firms in unrelated businesses, while at the same time managerial economies tend to encourage horizontal integration rather than diversification. Perhaps if it were not for this factor, all department store chains would be part of larger diversified conglomerates.

Why Firms Fail

Still more can be learned of successful management by studying management failure. W. T. Grant and Arlan's Department Stores furnish two classic examples of retail failure. Both were merchandising giants that expanded without the apparent management skill necessary to control their vast retail empires. Both concentrated heavily on price appeal, but, according to industry sources, neglected lines of communication between stores, suppliers, and managers. Internal coordination broke down almost completely in both cases. Other firms have barely managed to avoid failure by spending heavily to develop the cost controls and operating efficiency which were ignored by Grant's and Arlan's during their rapid expansions.

The incredible story of W. T. Grant may never be fully known, but what is public knowledge remains instructive for the rest of the industry. With 1,069 stores and a $51 million deficit, Grant's filed for bankruptcy in 1975, and became the largest retail failure in history. The reasons cited for its collapse are numerous, but the most significant concern the firm's inability to attract a large and loyal clientele, while new stores continued to open rapidly across the country. Thousands of pages of testimony by former executives and employees describe a company that suffered from a lack of internal communication and adequate budget and credit controls. According to testimony, store buyers were kept in the dark to such an extent that they often had to question outside vendors to determine Grant's own inventory levels. This led to massive inventory surpluses in some product lines which imposed a tremendous warehousing and interest cost on the company. In other product lines, customers were constantly frustrated by finding advertised specials out-of-stock. The lack of any systematic inventory control was exacerbated by the fact that the merchandise vice-president had no buying budget. This contributed to a rapid run-up in inventories before the company could put a stop on new vendor purchases.[11]

This was not the only trouble spot in the Grant's management structure. Coordination was so weak between central management and individual store managers that each store executive had to devise his own system of checking customer credit. As one might imagine, this led to credit card problems of enormous proportion. Moreover, as the situation at Grant's deteriorated, there was apparently an increase in white collar crime within the firm. According to the *Wall Street Journal*, Grant's buyers often requested vendors to deliberately overbill stores and later reimburse them personally for the amount of overpayment.[12]

History seems to suggest the existence of a slippery slope in the retail sector. Once a major firm begins to lose control over management, coordination rapidly disintegrates in a chain reaction leading to upward cost pressures. In a highly competitive industry, this quickly leads to a drop in profits and ultimately even to bankruptcy. The business is by nature decentralized, and therefore success lies mainly in the ability to coordinate far-flung operations. When this coordination breaks down, all appears to be lost.

The Arlan's department store chain provides another vivid example of a retail chain that failed, and for many of the same reasons. According to inside sources, Arlan's suffered from a leadership more concerned with outside interests than retailing. At a time when funds should have been invested in improving business operations, management spent lavishly on parties for employees to improve failing company morale. The more morale declined, the more lavish and desperate became the parties. Behind the desperation was a set of management decisions that could only be made by a company committed to expanding at any cost. According to one former executive of the firm, there was clearly an overemphasis on highly promotional merchandise which often sold for only a penny above cost; at the same time, there was an underemphasis on basic merchandise. This situation made competition with other discounters nearly impossible. Gross margins collapsed under this pressure leading to real income losses.

In the drive for "empire," Arlan's expanded to areas far from its central warehouse facilities, thus making the expense of shipping merchandise to these stores impractical. In its place, management instituted decentralized buying, but because of poor managerial communication, the result was a drop in product quality. This occurred despite management salaries rumored to be as high as $80,000 back in the early 1970's.

Near the end of its demise, Arlan's suffered the same indignities that faced W. T. Grant. Company buyers and executives lost all confidence in the firm. Some became notorious for overbuying merchandise and pocketing the difference. Inventory theft skyrocketed. By 1972, only a few short years after hitting its peak profit-level, Arlan's went bankrupt, closing all of its 107 stores. Ironically its last store to open—far from any central warehouse and clearly unprofitable—was in Waterloo, Iowa. Like Napoleon, expanding one's empire without careful advance planning can prove to be fatal.

The cases of W. T. Grant and Arlan's suggest that managerial blunders rather than external forces are the main cause of business failure among the larger chains. Yet no one should construe this as the major reason for failure among smaller independents. Except perhaps for the "mistake" of not selling out to a holding company, the high failure rate among independents can usually be traced to factors beyond the control of even the best management team. These include inadequate capital, a lack of scale economies, no access to quantity discounts, and central city location. The independents have become the victims of what the economist Joseph Schumpeter described as the process of "creative destruction"—the process by which private enterprise systems constantly create and destroy existing structures as a result of market forces.[13] Once the retail industry began on the road to centralization and expansion, it is hard to imagine that the independents could have survived in any number, no matter how perspicacious their management.

An Industry "Wish List"

Despite the enormous growth in the retail sector—particularly among chains and holding companies—retail trade executives are by no means completely satisfied with the "business climate" within which they operate. Like other corporate officials, they tend to blame a share of their problems on external factors, particularly government policy. When they are asked what changes in the "environment" would improve their ability to do business, their responses almost exclusively focus on the limitations imposed by government regulations. One retailer asserts, "my life is a continuing battle against government."[14]

Few retail executives believe they can improve operating efficiency through major new internal policies such as the development of on-the-job training or apprenticeship programs financed by the industry itself. No plans for the implementation of full scale training programs seem to be underway in the industry except for Caldor in New England. To improve profitability, department stores would prefer that the government initiate cost reductions through cuts in the minimum wage, reductions in taxes and utility rates, and relaxed restrictions on consumer credit.

Minimum wage legislation is the most often cited government restriction on the industry's freedom to operate as it would like. Government regulations—including those promulgated by ERISA (pensions), OSHA (safety), EEOC (equal opportunity), and the Magnuson-Moss Warranty Act, which requires that pre-sale warranty information be made available to customers ("no one ever asks for it," complains one retail chief)—are also prime targets of department store managers. They complain that the Federal government has saddled them with useless paperwork and that government "red tape" imposes unnecessary costs on their industry.

Also on the cost side, some managers lament regional taxes and the expense of utilities, especially in New England. For local firms, the effect of these costs is minimal; for the most part they affect all stores equally, and these costs, like wage costs, can be passed along to the consumer. The high cost of state taxes and utilities in regions like New England becomes important only in an inter-regional context, when regional branches of national companies must compete for funds with branches in other parts of the country. In these cases, high costs can make operations in one area less profitable, putting branches in the region at a disadvantage in their competition for investment capital.

Some executives also talk at length about what might be called the "anti-business" attitude of some state legislatures. "It's the oil companies that give us a bad name," one said in an interview. "Politically they [state legislators] lump all big business together. It hurts us." Among the legislatively imposed burdens he cites are state restrictions on the maximum level of interest which customers with overdue accounts can be charged. According to this industry source, the state ceiling is 3–6 percent below the rate which would allow his firm to "break even" on charge accounts. A few states also impose costs on firms when they require them to collect sales taxes without compensation for the administrative work involved. Many states do award such compensation, but many do not.

In addition to expressing their concerns about costs, department store executives often cite measures which they feel would increase sales and thereby improve the vitality of the industry. Topping the list is the elimination of Blue Laws, which industry sources believe would expand sales (by 5–6 percent according to one manager), rather than simply redistribute the same sales volume over a seven-day period. Some executives also speak in favor of the elimination or reduction of sales taxes, and some even suggest that income taxes should be increased if necessary in order to reduce sales and property taxes, both of which impose direct costs on the industry. Other executives want to see a revision of the Robinson-Patman Act, allowing large-scale firms even greater freedom to take advantage of quantity discounts.

Whether any of these concessions should be made to the industry is clearly a political question. Although some of these recommendations might increase the vitality of the department store sector as a whole, the overall political and economic costs associated with them need first to be thoroughly evaluated. Part of this evaluation must necessarily include normative judgments about the overall structure of retail trade. For example, is it worth doing anything to bolster the survival chances of smaller independents? If so, what costs are acceptable to assure this outcome? Moreover, one must consider how much the consumer should be protected, particularly from a retail sector that is increasingly concentrated in its ownership. How much should workers be protected in the industry, for example, through minimum wage legislation?

Clearly these are all policy questions that will inevitably continue to lie at the crux of department store debates. The outcome of such debates plays an enormous role in the future structuring of the industry and how consumers obtain goods and services through the distribution network in the nation.

Endnotes

1. "Federated Department Stores" (Boston: Harvard Business School, Intercollegiate Case Clearing House, No. 375-147), p. 16.
2. *Ibid.*
3. "Federated . . . and the Consumer Comeback," *Dun's Review* (December 1967), p. 38.
4. "Federated Department Stores" *op. cit.*, p. 17.
5. William R. Davidson, Albert D. Bates, and Stephen J. Bass, "The Retail Life Cycle," *Harvard Business Review* (November–December 1976), p. 95.
6. "Federated . . . and the Consumer Comeback," *op. cit.*, p. 39.
7. "Federated Department Stores," *op. cit.*, p. 11.
8. "Profile on Zayre," *Discount Merchandiser* (June 1978), p. 12.
9. "Big Oil's Move into Retailing," *Chain Store Age Executive* (September 1976), p. 29.
10. *Ibid.*
11. Stanley H. Slom, "Grant Testimony Shows It Lacked Curbs on Budget, Credit and Had Internal Woes," *The Wall Street Journal* (February 4, 1977).
12. *Ibid.*
13. Joseph Shumpeter, *Capitalism, Socialism, and Democracy,* 3rd ed. (New York: Harper and Row, 1942).
14. David A. Loehwing, "Trouble in the Store," *Barrons* (July 21, 1969), p. 3.

Selected Sources

William R. Davidson, Albert D. Bates, and Stephen J. Bass, "The Retail Life Cycle,"
  Harvard Business Review (November–December 1976).
"Federated Department Stores" Boston, Mass.: Harvard Business School, Intercol-
  legiate Case Clearing House, No. 375-147.
David A. Loehwing, "Trouble in the Store." *Barrons* (July 21, 1969).
Joseph Schumpeter, *Capitalism, Socialism, and Democracy*, 3rd ed. (New York:
  Harper and Row, 1942).

Chapter 9

SUMMARY AND CONCLUSION

As America became a "consumer society" in the twentieth century, it was perhaps inevitable that the strength of its retail sector would expand to rival the economic power of its manufacturing base. We have seen the department store industry undergo a dramatic transformation in order to fulfill this role. As recently as the 1930's retail trade was the province of the small, family-owned business which served a local market in an informal personal style. From these *petite-bourgeoisie* roots have grown the rapidly evolving national and international corporate enterprises which today dominate the industry. The thorough restructuring of retail trade, brought about by a combination of economic, demographic, institutional, and legislative forces, has enormous implication for consumer welfare, for labor, and for local and regional economies. The distribution sector is no longer the poor stepchild in the national economy.

The "Industrialization" of Department Stores

Changes in the structure of the department store industry recall in many respects changes which took place in the manufacturing sector a generation or two ago. Increased concentration in ownership, the growth of centralized financial control, the development of a corporate managerial hierarchy, an effort to reduce the skill requirements in the labor force, the substitution of capital for labor, and the emergence of giant firms which are able to buy out or drive out their competition are all familiar phenomena to those who have studied the development of the manufacturing base. The "industrialization" of retail trade, through changes in structure and strategy which parallel those in manufacturing, is not yet so familiar a story.

143

The recent history of the department store industry, however, suggests that the same forces which have transformed so many other sectors of the economy are at work in retail trade as well.

A series of developments in merchandising methods—the "modes of production" of retail services—have fostered the consolidation of ownership and the growth of giant retail firms during the last half-century. One should recall that the development of the department store was itself a consolidation, bringing together in one place and under one management merchandise previously available only through unrelated specialty shops. This was followed by a movement to bring together department stores around the country under one corporate umbrella. The national holding company was designed as a buffer against the risk faced in individual local markets and as a conduit for the exchange of advice and information. The emergence of the discount store in the 1950's further restructured the industry by undercutting department store prices and forcing the more established retailing modes to cut costs or to compete on a basis other than price. The rise of the chain store, both full-price and discount, permitted the large firms to exploit tremendous economies of scale, and in so doing to grow even larger. In turn, these large chains became incorporated, developed a sophisticated management style, and left behind the trappings and attitudes of the small, provincial businesses from which they sprang. Ultimately, the largest retail corporations became conglomerated, in many cases moving out of the retail industry to acquire interests in manufacturing, insurance, real estate, fast food, and other industries.

The largest retail firms, those which have grown to dominate the industry, have arrived at a stage where they blend in with the corporate landscape. Department stores are now not uncommonly multinational, multibillion dollar concerns, wooing graduates of the most prestigious business schools to their management teams and rewarding them with competitive salaries. Leaving behind the local market, with its regional peculiarities and its microcosmic concerns, giant retail corporations now move in a national and even international capital market. Investment decisions, formerly based on the availability of local capital and the economic conditions prevailing in the region, are now made with the nation and the world as the relevant arena. Local branches now compete for investment capital with stores located in distant places. While this wide scope of operations permits capital to be invested where it will earn the greatest private return, it often results in the draining of profits from branches which show a slightly lower earnings rate. Such earnings as are made in the less profitable regions of the country are not being reinvested in the immediate area but are being transferred instead to other parts of the country and the world. When the parent firm is part of a large national or international network, local communities lose control of their capital base. This situation is not unlike that of communities in the Midwest whose economic base consisted of multinational auto, steel, and rubber enterprises.

A further consequence of the growth of the large corporate firm is the attenuation of managerial commitment, not just to a particular region but to the retail industry as a whole. While it has generally been true that the heads of merchandise corporations tended to stay within the retail sector when expanding or acquiring other firms, the barriers to expansion outside the industry appear to be breaking down. K-Mart, for example, rather than settling for decreasing profits in an increasingly saturated retail market, is contemplating systematic acquisitions in other sectors, just as conglomerates which have grown from bases in manufacturing or extraction industries have done. It appears, then, that even individual store branches will face growing head-to-head competition with holdings in other industries when they seek investment capital from their parent company.

Yet for all the similarity between giant retail enterprises and the traditional powers that be in the manufacturing sector, there continue to be some clear differences between these two sectors. One of these is the fierce price-based competition that persists in the department store industry regardless of the degree of sales concentration. With the expansion of the market for consumer goods, the development of national merchandising chains, and the use of the electronic and print media to create conditions not unlike the "perfect information" assumptions of classical economic theory, competition has intensified. The growing saturation of the retail market, particularly in the Northeast and the Pacific regions, has increased competitive pressure to the point that some firms, in the rush to preempt choice retail locations, take the risk of building highly leveraged empires which prove to be unsustainable. For many of these firms, "grow or die" has become "grow *and* die" as profit margins erode and finally disappear. Retail saturation forces all firms into a constant search for new ways to cut costs. Raising prices, as in the auto or steel industry, is simply not an available strategy in the retail sector.

Despite emerging oligopoly in the department store industry, price competition shows no sign of abating at this time. If anything, the existence of giant firms which can afford extensive advertising and which consider themselves to be in direct competition with each other has escalated the price war. It seems likely that as consolidation continues and the oligopolistic structure of the industry becomes more pronounced, some form of explicit price leadership will develop among the largest firms. But this is still in the future. Because retail is not particularly capital-intensive, and because there will always be room—at least at the local level—for a firm with a "better concept," it is highly unlikely that the industry will ever reach full oligopoly. Nevertheless, at the highest levels the trend toward large, centralized corporate structures which eclipse their smaller competitors is continuing apace.

Advertising, Technology, and Government Policy: Returns to Bigness

The growth of large firms at the expense of small retail outlets has been encouraged by three forces, all of which have expanded the ability of retail giants to operate more profitably than their small competitors. Advertising and computerized technology provide substantial economies of scale, while government policy, intended to protect the small merchant from competitive erosion of profit margins, has sometimes had the opposite effect.

Large department stores, both discount and full-price, have come to rely heavily on advertising, particularly through the electronic media, to give the sales pitch formerly given by a trained salesperson. Particularly when stores are clustered in one geographic region, advertising can provide tremendous economies of scale by publicizing the product and reducing the need for a large, trained sales force in individual stores. Computerized technology, particularly that designed to improve inventory control, can also generate tremendous savings. Combined, they provide an almost unbeatable competitive edge.

The enormous costs of mass advertising and electronic technology, in effect, form a barrier to entry into the mass market. A retail firm must achieve a considerable size before it can afford to use those methods which will enable it to grow still larger. Advertising and electronic data processing equipment thus contribute to uneven development in the industry, accelerating the growth of already large businesses and handicapping those too small to afford the large outlays of cash required.

Ironically, advertising, which gives the largest retailers a substantial competitive edge, also exacerbates price competition among the large firms. Few businesses can afford a full-color supplement to the Sunday newspaper, but those who can are certain to have their prices and offerings compared with those of other firms which advertise in the same way. Consumers obviously benefit from the resulting price wars between large retailers and from having easy access to price information. Whether the costs, in the form of reduced sales staff at the store, centralized decisions over product mix, and the gradual disappearance of small independents, outweigh these benefits is a matter of personal judgment.

Government policy has also played a role—at some times accelerating and at other times retarding—the transformation of the retail sector. Fair trade laws were for many years effective in limiting the role of the discounter by requiring that certain items be sold only at a manufacturer's set price. It was not until these laws were repealed or left unenforced that discounting became a serious challenge to traditional merchandising. Similarly the Robinson-Patman Act sought to protect small firms which bought their merchandise through a broker from the competitive advantage of the large firm which could buy without an intermediary. There is evidence that loopholes in the act permitted manufacturers to circumvent the law by excluding the smaller firm altogether. Thus the effect of the law differed from its original intent, in some cases actually contributing to the demise of the independent.

Both fair trade laws and the Robinson-Patman Act are products of Depression-era protectionism. The fact that independent retailers support modification, not repeal, of the Robinson-Patman Act suggests that despite its perversity it has still been of some benefit to small business. One need only observe that independents have been the major casualties of the discount boom to realize that the legislative efforts of the 1930's were at least partially effective in protecting small merchants.

Repeal of protectionist legislation, while clearly benefiting big business and hurting the independent, is nevertheless a boon to consumers, at least in the short-run. Allowing unfettered competition on the basis of price has clear advantages for the largest retailers who can take full advantage of the cost savings their size permits. Measures which keep prices down naturally benefit consumers. Yet increased market concentration, reduced store variety, the drainage of capital from older regions, and the demise of the independent may not be in the consumers' long-term interest. How this all turns out is yet to be seen.

Transformation of the Labor Market and the Labor Process

Changes as dramatic as those in the structure of the department store industry can hardly fail to have an impact on the industry's demand for labor and on the labor process itself. In the past two decades alone there has been a significant change in the age composition of the workforce, in the wage structure of the industry, and in the sorts of employment opportunities which the industry offers. Each of these is a result of fierce interfirm competition and the transition to complex corporate forms of management.

In the brief period since the mid–1950's, a surprisingly distinct dual labor structure has evolved within the industry. It contains at the top of the hierarchy a stratum of highly skilled managerial jobs and at the bottom a profuse number of low-paid, unskilled slots. The new hierarchy is reflected in a polarized wage structure and a diverging skill mix. Near-minimum wages which are the norm in the industry stand in sharp contrast to the six-figure annual earnings of top management. Administrative sophistication within the executive suites has increased enormously since the days of the small, independent department store, while sales and clerical slots have increasingly been turned into unskilled, part-time jobs. As a result, the industry is now characterized by a "missing middle" in its skill structure.

The vast majority of jobs in the department store industry conform to the definition of the typical slot in the secondary labor market. Skill requirements are low or nonexistent, little training is done by the employer, wages are near the legal minimum, and work is usually available only on a part-time basis. The turnover rate among employees is mushrooming as skill requirements are undermined and as fewer department store jobs promise long-term career-caliber employment.

This deskilling of the labor force has been achieved by the substitution of technological innovations, particularly the electronic media, for labor. Today it is the television commercial, the radio spot or the Sunday newspaper supplement that sells the product, not the department store employee. The sales clerk who knows the product well is a vanishing breed. Except in some specialty shops and a few full-price department stores, the trained salesperson has been replaced by "order-takers" who know little more about their jobs than how to use a cash register. The cash register, too, has been simplified, so that many stores now use automatic checkout devices which substantially reduce the number of steps involved in ringing up a sale.

One result of deskilling, and the competitive pressure to reduce fringe benefit costs by reducing full-time work, is a dramatic compositional change in the industry's labor force. Women and youth, whether by choice or because of a lack of alternative employment opportunity, now comprise the bulk of department store employment, and those who can find more stable, high-paying employment look elsewhere. White men generally hold the well-paid managerial slots. Except for a few high-paying positions at the top, the industry no longer provides "careers"; it provides only jobs. It has, as a result, become a relatively inappropriate channel for economic development and a dead-end street for many job-seekers. Even industry sources see this as an unfortunate aspect of the retail revolution.

The Future of the Department Store Industry

What then of the future? Will the industry continue to follow in the historical footsteps of the manufacturing sector, finding a method to quell price competition and "rationalize" the industry? Or will new forms of trade tend to undermine the power of the large retailers and return us to a period of smaller shops and greater competition? Will the skilled salesperson return to this industry, making trade a more personal service to the consumer and more satisfying to the worker? Or will the salesworker be displaced altogether? These are all causes for speculation.

The flourishing specialty store in the new suburban malls and on fashionable downtown streets appears to indicate a trend counter to the development of the massive department store and concentrated ownership. Yet even here the specialty store is part of the unfolding corporate strategy. Behind most of these specialty shops is now a large corporation which uses the chain specialty store to penetrate markets previously inaccessible to it. As these chain stores jockey for position in an increasingly saturated retail market, it is not unlikely that competition will abate as remaining retail locations are exhausted.

Once the tempestuous forces of the retail boom subside, retail may well follow the lead of other industries which have experienced waves of consolidation. With battles for retail turf resolved, price leadership is likely to develop among the largest firms. This can be expected to result in a rise in consumer prices over the long run. It will also mark the full maturity of the retail sector and will, in many ways, make it indistinguishable from the traditional manufacturing industries that dominate commerce in advanced nations.

One of the consequences of the tremendous success of the large chain store will be an inevitable trend toward standardization in both retailing style and in the merchandise offered in the marketplace. Central buying, even in stores which allow managers a degree of local autonomy, insures that all stores in a chain will offer similar products. While the amount and variety of merchandise today is vastly greater than at the turn of the century, centralized mass purchasing may eventually have the effect of reducing the range of products available. By ordering merchandise in enormous quantities, the largest chains may develop the market power to assure the success of some suppliers and the demise of others. The tables may ultimately turn with the manufacturing sector playing stepchild to the retail giants. It seems reasonable to expect that concentration in the retail industry will be echoed in concentration among suppliers, since the market power of the largest chains is sufficient to determine which suppliers survive. Thus, to an ever greater extent, it may become the retail merchant, not the consumer, who is sovereign in the marketplace.

There is also an important spatial dimension to this forecast. The merchandiser's direct dependence on population and regional income levels insures that, despite uneven development in the structure of ownership in the industry, its spatial evolution will tend to be an equalizing force between regions. The ascendency of national ownership patterns is hastening the transfer of profits from older, more saturated regions to younger, booming areas of the nation and the world. While retail trade cannot lead the economic development of a region, it can clearly exacerbate a region's economic decline. When a nationally set standard of profitability, dominates any commitment to a specific locale or community, the stage is set for accelerated capital mobility and a rapid ratification of reinvestment decisions made in the leading manufacturing sectors of each region. Department stores can "move" as fast—or faster—than manufacturing firms.

Moreover, in saturated areas of the country, and eventually in the nation as a whole, the outlook for new store construction and for an expansion in retail employment is quite gloomy. The saturation of many areas of the United States insures that in those regions there will be no boom in employment similar to that in New England in the 1960's. Any growth in the number of workers employed in the industry will be the result of increasing part-time employment, with no gain in the total number of hours worked. Ultimately, employment may even decline as firms pare their staffs in an attempt to further reduce the costs of doing business.

Indeed, this trend can be seen in the latest moves by retailing giants such as Montgomery Ward. In mid–1980, Ward's announced that it would convert 100 of its stores in the East and the Mid-West to "Jefferson Ward" self-service outlets over a period of three years. The move is explicitly aimed at reducing labor costs. According to a company spokesman, the Jefferson stores employ "substantially fewer" people per store than their regular retail outlets.[1] At the same time, the company is further reducing employment by centralizing its management activities. The supervision of its retail stores will be centralized in Chicago and its regional staff functions in Chicago, Dallas, and Oakland, California are to be eliminated. Technology has made this all possible. According to Ward's chairman, the elimination of regional staffs was made feasible "by the successful computerization of our retail operating and merchandizing functions."[2]

Employment expansion may still occur in areas not yet saturated with retail trade, but once the saturation point is reached, development will halt in those regions as well. At that point the locus of new investment will shift to other industries and to other parts of the world. It is a sobering forecast, suggesting something not far different from what has already occurred in the core manufacturing sectors of the United States.

The forecast may be even more sobering, at least for those who are concerned about employment levels, product variety, and the continued survival of small enterprise. The current revolution in telecommunications may make the department store all but obsolete. Interactive cable television is just beginning on an experimental basis to bring department store shopping into the living room. If these experiments, along with the automated warehouse, prove successful, we can look forward to the day when not only the experienced salesperson but even the unskilled cashier and the stock clerk will disappear from the retail scene. At that point a handful of mammoth corporations will be left to constitute the distributive network in the nation. Such a 21st century forecast is by no means unreasonable. It is something that the industry as well as trade unionists and government planners will have to face. Behind the glitter and glamor of the modern department store is a saga of dramatic change and adaptation that we are only beginning to comprehend.

Endnotes

1. "Montgomery Ward to Convert 100 Units," *New York Times* (August 1, 1980), p. D4.
2. *Ibid.*

BIBLIOGRAPHY

Advertising Age, "Middle, Upper-Middle Income Families Buy from Discounters, Cleveland Press Finds" (January 16, 1967).

American Bankers Association, *Statistical Abstract of the United States, 1977*. Washington, D.C.: United States Government Printing Office, 1977.

Blumenthal, Ralph. "Legal Problems for Discounters." *The New York Times* (February 2, 1979).

Boston Globe, "Retail Heavies in the Hub" (April 1, 1979).

Boston Globe, "Shifting Gears with $18b Sears" (February 18, 1979).

Business Week, "In Business this Week" (November 27, 1978).

Business Week, "Much Ado . . . States Drop Fair-Trade Laws, but Impact Is Small" (February 17, 1975).

Business Week, "Saving the Company that Acquired Him" (February 19, 1979).

Business Week, "Will Congress End Fair Trade?" (February 17, 1975).

Caldor 1977 Annual Report, "To Our Shareholders" (April 12, 1978).

Carruth, Eleanore. "K-Mart Has To Open Some New Doors on the Future," *Fortune* (July, 1977).

Chain Store Age (General Merchandise Edition), "Future Shock/Marketing: A New Role for Buyers–Sellers" (September, 1975).

Chain Store Age Executive, "Big Oil's Move into Retailing" (September 1976).

Chandler, Alfred D. *Strategy & Structure*. Cambridge, Mass.: M I T Press 1962.

Cole, Robert J. "Prime Takeover Target: Insurance Companies," *The New York Times* (May 29, 1979).

Davidson, William R., Albert D. Bates, and Stephen J. Bass. "The Retail Life Cycle," *Harvard Business Review* (November–December, 1976).

Department Store Retailing in an Era of Change. Washington, D.C.: U.S. Department of Commerce, Domestic and International Business Administration.

Discount Merchandiser. (March 1967).

Discount Merchandiser, "President's Survey—Review of a Rough Year and Prospects for 1975" (December 1974).

Discount Merchandiser, "S.S. Kresge's Chairman Talks on Discounting" (January 1978).

Discount Merchandiser, "The True Look of the Discount Industry" (May 1960–1978).

Discount Store News, "Bradlees: 6 Units in '61 Before Sales to Stop & Shop" Vol. 11, No. 6 (December 11, 1972).

Discount Store News, "Discountland Marches from $6b to $26.15b." Vol. 11, No. 26 (December 11, 1972).

Discount Store News, "Food Folk went Discount from Scratch to Catch," Vol. 11, No. 26 (December 11, 1972).

Discount Store News, "Garb Men Sprouted Discount Branches Way Back," Vol. 11, No. 26 (December 11, 1972).

Discount Store News, "Many Discounters Defy New York State Blue Law," Vol. 11, No. 26 (December 11, 1972).

Discount Store News, "Origins of the Chains: The Innovators," Vol. 11, No. 26 (December 11, 1972).

Discount Store News, "The Pioneers of Discountland," Vol. 11, No. 26 (December 11, 1972).

Discount Store News, "70's—a Decade for Individuality," Vol. 11, No. 26 (December 11, 1972).

Discount Store News, "Ten Years of Discount Retailing," Vol. 11, No. 26 (December 11, 1972).

Duncan, Delbert I., and Stanley C. Hollander. *Modern Retailing Management.* Homewood, Ill.: Richard D. Irwin, Inc. 1977.

Dun's Review. "Federated . . . and the Consumer Comeback." December 1967.

Fairchild's Financial Manual of Retail Stores. New York: Fairchild Publications. 1963–1978.

"Federated Department Stores." Boston: Harvard Business School, Intercollegiate Case Clearing House. No. 8-375-304, rev. June 1975.

Forbes Magazine, "How Much Does *Your* Boss Make?" (June 11, 1979).

Govindarajan, Vijayaraghavan. "Sears, Roebuck and Company: A Historical Background." Boston: Harvard Business School, Intercollegiate Case Clearing House, No. 4-179-123, rev. February 1979.

Lenzer, Robert. "Massive Shakeup Yields Dividend," *Boston Globe* (April 12, 1979).

Loehwing, David A. "Discounters Discounted: Nobody Likes Them Any More But the Customers," *Barrons* (April 22, 1963).

——— "Trouble in the Store," *Barrons* (July 21, 1969).

McClelland, W. G. "The United Kingdom" in J. J. Boddewyn and S. C. Hollander, eds., *Public Policy toward Retailing.* Lexington, Massachusetts: Lexington Books. 1972.

Mahoney, Tom and Leonard Sloane. *The Great Merchants.* New York: Harper & Row. 1974.

Miracle, Gordon E. "Sears, Roebuck and Company, Brazil (A)." Boston: Intercollegiate Case Clearing House, No. 9-572-624, 1971.

Moeser, D. E. "Sound Buying Practices," *The Buyer's Manual* (1972).

Moody's Investors Service, *Moody's Industrial Manual*. New York 1978.

Morgan, Gwynne. "Retail Heavies Struggle in the Hub," *Boston Globe* (April 1, 1979).

New York Times Magazine, "Department Store as Theatre" (April 29, 1979).

Ney, J. M. *The Buyer's Manual*, 4th edition. New York: National Retail Merchants Association, 1965.

Slom, Stanley H. "Grant Testimony Shows It Lacked Curbs on Budget, Credit and Had Internal Woes," *Wall Street Journal* (February 14, 1977).

Star, Steven H. "Sears, Roebuck and Company." Boston: Harvard Business School, Intercollegiate Case Clearing House, No. 6-570-040: M 386, 1963 and 1969.

Streeter, Bill. "White House Eyeing Robinson-Patman Act; Repeal Is Possible," *Industrial Distribution* (November 1975).

Tarpey, Lawrence X. "Buyer Liability Under Robinson-Patman Act," *Journal of Marketing*. Vol. 36 (January 1972).

Tuhy, Carrie. "Boston: An Old Grey Lady Finds the Secret of Youth," *Daily News Record* (March 1979).

U.S. Bureau of Economic Analysis, *Survey of Current Business* (August 1973 and April 1974).

U.S. Bureau of the Census, *Census of Retail Trade*, 1963, 1967, 1972, and 1977. Washington, D.C.: U.S. Government Printing Office.

U.S. Bureau of the Census, *Monthly Retail Trade Reports*, 1967–1977. Washington, D.C.: U.S. Government Printing Office.

U.S. Bureau of the Census, *United States Census of Business: 1948*, Vols. I, IV, VI. Washington, D.C.: U.S. Government Printing Office, 1966.

U.S. Bureau of the Census, *Estimates and Projections of the Population of States: 1970 to 2000*, Washington, D.C.: U.S. Government Printing Office, March 1974.

U.S. Bureau of the Census, *Number, Median Income, and Standard Errors in 1975 and 1969 of Families and Unrelated Individuals Based on the Survey of Income and Education (SIE) and the 1970 Census for Regions, Divisions,and States*, Washington, D.C.: U.S. Government Printing Office, 1977.

U.S. Bureau of the Census, *Population Estimates and Projections*, Series P-25, No. 735. Washington, D.C.: U.S. Government Printing Office, October 1978.

U.S. Bureau of the Census, *United States Census of Population: 1970*, Vol. I. Washington, D.C.: U.S. Government Printing Office, 1970.

U.S. Bureau of the Census, *1977 Census of Retail Trade*.

U.S. Department of Commerce, *Department Store Retailing in an Era of Change*, 1975. Washington, D.C.: U.S. Government Printing Office, 1975.

U.S. Department of Commerce, *Food from Farmer to Consumer*. Washington, D.C.: U.S. Government Printing Office, 1966.

INDEX

Abraham & Strauss, 11, 15, 24
Advanced technology: *see* Technology
Advertising, 3, 6, 18, 20, 25–26, 65,
    115–16, 146–47
Age, in labor force, 80, 83–84,
    90–91, 95–96, 149
  and wages, 99–102, 104–105,
    107–108
Allied Stores Corporation, 23–24, 32,
    51
Arlan's, 13, 31, 53–54, 67, 137–39
Army-Navy stores, 13
Associated Merchandising
    Corporation (AMC)(1918), 11

Bankruptcy, 31, 52, 54, 67, 137–39
Bargain basements, 11–12, 32, 71
Birch, David, 8
Bloomingdale's, 15, 24–25
Blue Laws, 129–31, 140
Bradlees, 12, 14, 19, 73, 110
Brooke, Edward, 125

Caldor, 12, 19, 65, 111, 139
Capital, and retail industry, 66–70,
    77, 133, 146
"Cash-cow status," 69
Central city markets, 72; *see also*
    Location
Centralized buying systems, 64–65,
    121–22, 135, 150
Chase, Marty, 12, 36
Coffman, Max, 13

Commission selling, decline in,
    109–10
Competition, 2–3, 14, 145–47
  effect of corporate structure on, 69
  and discount stores, 19, 23, 36
  management's role and, 133–34
  and market saturation, 55, 60
  and profit trends, 51
  specialty stores and, 27–29
  struggle between retail modes and,
    29–32
  technology use and, 113
  and unions, 110
Computers, 112–14, 146, 151; *see*
    also Technology
Consolidation, 2–3, 23, 47–50,
    144–46, 149–50
Consumer credit, 36, 46–47
Consumer markets, 15, 17–19, 20,
    28, 31–34, 44–46
Corporate ownership, 61–66, 77,
    112, 150
  effect on competition, 69–70, 77
Costs, 118–19, 140
  advertising, 146
  computers, 114
  control, 62–64, 66, 150
  of fringe benefits, 27, 149
  of labor, 106–109, 151
  transportation, 113
County Business Patterns, 83

Day, William, 125
Dayton-Hudson Corporation, 23–25,
    32, 119

Deep South region, 40
Demographic factors, 14, 34, 36–43
Department store industry
  changes in, 1–3, 143–46
  definition of, 3–4, 15
  future of, 149–51
  history of, 1, 10–15, 29
  impact on labor, 3, 6, 80–82,
      117–19, 148–49
  structure of, 2–7, 16–18, 20, 29,
      143–46, 151
"Deskilling," 98, 105, 108–109,
  116–19, 148–49
Discount department store chains, 4,
  6, 8, 11–15, 18–23, 50–51, 119,
  144; *see also* Bargain basements
  and Blue Laws, 130
  and fair trade laws, 125–27
  and labor costs, 108
  management in, 134–36
  specialty store acquisitions by, 33
  and struggle between retail modes,
    29–32
Discount Merchandiser, 67
Discount Store News, 23
Disposable income, 36, 46, 57
Distribution, 65, 113, 128–29
Diversification, 2, 4, 32, 74–76,
  136–37, 144
Dual labor market, 98, 105
Dun & Bradstreet, 8, 50, 58

Earnings: *see* Wages
Economic factors, 14, 34, 36, 44–
  46
Economies of scale, 64–65, 144,
  146
EDP: *see* Electronic data processing
EEOC, 140
Electronic data processing (EDP),
  18, 23, 25, 27, 29, 112–13
Employee: *see* Labor force
Employment, 37, 59–60, 80–82,
  117–19, 150–51
  and market saturation, 80–82
ERISA, 139–40
Expansion: *see* Growth patterns

Fair trade laws, 18, 20, 33, 124–28,
  131, 147
Faneuil Hall Marketplace, 71
Federal Trade Commission, 124
Federated Department Stores, 11,
  15, 23, 24, 32, 48–49, 51, 66,
  70, 134–35
Filene, Lincoln, 11, 36
Filene's, 10–12, 15, 24–25, 70–71, 74
Forbes, 103
Fox, G., 24, 73
Fringe benefits, 27, 108–11, 149
Full-time equivalent (FTE)
  employment, 27, 83, 103–104,
  108

Gold Circle, 15, 19, 24, 32
Gold Key, 15, 24, 32
Gold Triangle, 15, 24, 32
Government policy, and retail
  industry, 3, 14, 36, 120, 131–32,
  139–40, 146–47
  Blue Laws, 129–31
  recent legislation, 128–29
  Resale Price Maintenance, 124–28
  Robinson-Patman Act, 120–24
Grant, W. T., 31, 54, 67, 137–39
Gross margins, definition of, 13
Grover-Cronin, 10–11, 32, 62, 75
Growth patterns, of retail industry
  into central city markets, 72
  employment growth within, 80–82
  into international markets, 76–77,
    145
  methods of, 72–74
  into nonretail areas, 74–76, 126
  and ownership type, 63–64, 70–74
  and retained earnings, 66–68
  into suburban markets, 70–71

Harvard Business Review, 134
Hit Or Miss, 15

Income, 17, 20, 33, 36, 44–46, 57,
  150; *see also* Disposable income

Independent department stores, 4,
6–7, 8, 10–11, 50–52, 147
growth patterns of, 73
and national holding companies, 25
ownership, 61–64, 112, 150
and Robinson-Patman Act, 124
Industrial structure, of retail
industry, 2–6, 143–46
International markets, 3, 9, 69–70,
76–77, 145
Investment, changes in, 66–68, 77,
144

J.M. Fields, 14, 110
Jordan Marsh, 24, 70–71

Kings Department Store, 13, 19
K-Mart, 19–20, 49, 59, 63–69, 113,
119, 133, 135–36, 145
expansion, 74–75
Krensky, Harold, 134

Labor force, 3, 80–82, 148–49
changes in demand for, 80–82,
117–19
costs, 106–109, 151
deskilling, 98, 105, 108–109,
116–19, 148–49
destination of, 89–92
dual labor market, 98, 105
mobility of, 88, 92–97
part-time, 27, 82–84, 95–96, 99,
103–105, 108–109, 148
and retail modes of production,
6–7, 15, 18, 20, 25, 27–28
skilled vs. unskilled, 80, 83–86,
90–91, 96, 98–99, 104, 108,
111, 116, 119, 148–49
source of, 87–89, 148
effects of technology on, 112–15
training for, 64, 111–12, 139, 148
effect of transportation and
advertising on, 115–16
turnover and tenure, 84–86,
111–12, 148

wages, 87, 98–106, 117–19, 135,
144–45, 148
Labor markets, secondary vs.
primary, 87–90, 95, 148
Lazarus, Ralph, 11, 135
Lazarus & Company, F.R., 11, 24,
135
Leasing, 13, 33
Lechmere Sales, 25, 32
LEED file, 8, 84, 87, 99, 107
Legislation, effect on retail industry,
120–31, 147
Local factors, 69–70, 77, 143–45, 150
Location, and retail modes, 20, 26,
28, 31, 70–72, 76–77, 115, 133,
149; *see also* Central city
markets, International markets,
Suburban markets
Longitudinal Employer-Employee
Data file: *see* LEED file

Magnuson-Moss Warranty Act, 140
Mammoth Mart, 13
Management
changes for, 139–41
failure of, 137–39
training programs for, 64, 111–12
and unions, 111
wages and, 101–103, 135
Management structures
changes in goals and style of, 1, 4,
143–46, 151
of retail modes, 6–7, 16–18, 20, 29
Market concentration, 47–50
Markets, 54–60
central city, 72
consumer, 15, 17–20, 28, 31–34
international, 3, 9, 69–70, 76–77,
145
labor, 87–90, 95, 148
nonretail, 74–76
suburban, 70–71, 115
Market saturation, 34, 145, 150
effect on employment, 80–81
and expansion, 70
and retail markets, 54–60
Marty's Clothing Mart, 12

Maxx Shops, T.J., 15
May Department Stores Company,
    23–24, 73
McCracken, Paul, 63
Medi-Mart, 14
Men, in retail labor force, 88–89,
    91–92, 95–96, 149
  wages for, 99–103, 105
Merchandise line, 15–16, 18–19, 20,
    26, 28, 33, 65
Mid-Atlantic region, 37, 42, 44–45,
    54, 68
Minimum wage, 99, 106–109,
    139–40, 148
Mobility, 90–97
Modes of production, 4–7, 15–29,
    134–36, 144, 147; *see also*
    Department store chains,
    Discount department store
    chains, Independent department
    stores, National holding
    companies, Specialty stores
  deskilling, 109–10, 116
  and fair trade laws, 125–28
  growth of, 49–51, 75–77
  integration, 74–75
  and Robinson-Patman Act, 122–24
  struggles between, 29–34
Montgomery-Ward, 15, 17, 34, 52,
    73, 76, 136, 150–51
"Moonlighting," 91
Mountain region, 37, 40, 42, 44–45,
    57

National Commission on Marketing,
    124
National holding companies, 4, 6, 8,
    15, 23–25, 49–51, 144
  and capital, 67–69
  growth patterns of, 73–74, 77
  and independents, 25
  retained earnings, 67
  and Robinson-Patman Act, 121–22
National markets, 36–46, 145
  and discount stores, 14, 19–20
  vs. local markets, 2–3, 6, 8–9,
    69–70, 77

National Small Business Association,
    124
Net income/sales ratio, 51–54; *see
    also* Profits
*New England Census of Retail
    Trade*, 117
New England region, 8, 12–13,
    37–42, 140, 145, 150
  Blue Laws in, 129–30
  capital movement in, 68–69
  market saturation in, 54–56,
    58–59, 81–82
  and ownership modes, 50–51
  per capita income in, 44–45
Nonretail firms, 32, 74–76; *see also*
    Diversification, Oil companies,
    Sears
North-Central region, 37–40, 42,
    44–45, 68

Oil companies, in retail industry, 34,
    76, 136, 140
Oiligopoly, retail, 2, 145–46
OSHA, 140
Ownership patterns, 2, 6–7, 11, 14,
    26–28, 36, 47–49
  economies of scale and, 64–66,
    146–47
  and legislation, 128
  private vs. corporate, 61–64, 112,
    150
  and regional growth/decline, 50–51

Pacific region, 37, 40, 44–45, 57, 68,
    145
Palestine, Lester, 13, 36
Part-time labor, 27, 82–84, 95–96,
    99, 103–105, 108–109, 148
Payroll/sales ratio, 6–7, 18, 20, 25,
    27–28, 50, 108–109, 117–19
Penney, J.C., 15, 32, 48, 52
Per capita income, 44–46
Point-of-sale technology, 113–14
Population growth, 36–43, 56–59,
    150
Price/earnings ratio, 63, 76

Price fixing, 128–29
Prices, 28, 145–47
  and discount stores, 16, 18–19, 31
  and fair trade laws, 124–28
  and management style, 135–36
  and Robinson-Patman Act, 120–24
Private ownership, 61–64, 73, 77
Productivity, 112–15, 117–19
Profits, 16–17, 117, 119, 144–45, 150
  of independents, 26–27
  and retained earnings, 66–68
  trends in, 51–54, 69–70, 74
Profit/sales margin, 51–54, 133

Quantity discounts, 121–23

Race, and wages, 99, 101
Recession, 36, 81–82, 118
Regions, 144–45, 150–51
  and capital movement, 68–70
  department store growth/decline,
    50–51
  and market saturation, 54–60
  per capita income, 44–46
  population growth in, 37–42
Resale Price Maintenance, 124–28
Retail Clerks International, 110–11
Retail Clerks Union: *see* United
    Food and Commercial Workers
    of America
Retail Research Associates
    (RRA)(1916), 11
Retained earnings, 27, 66–68
Return on investment (ROI), 16–17
Robinson-Patman Price
    Discrimination Act (1936), 65,
    120–21, 131, 140, 147

Sales, 1, 4, 117–18; *see also* Payroll/
    sales ratio
  and labor, 18, 108
  and ownership, 48–50
  /profits ratio, 51–54, 133
  and retail modes of production,
    13–15, 18, 20

Schoenberg Mercantile Company, 23
Sears, 15–17, 48, 65, 74–75, 77, 126
  diversification, 32, 74
Sex, and wages, 99–105, *see also*
    Men, Women
Simon, Franklin, 70
Size, changes in, 57, 146–47
  and capital movement, 68–70
  legislation's effect on, 122, 124–26,
    130–32
  and ownership, 62, 64–66
Sony v. Horst A. Eiberger of
    Atlanta, 129
South Atlantic region, 37, 40, 42, 44
Specialty stores, 1, 4–5, 7, 10,
    12–14, 27–29, 149
  fair trade laws' effect on, 127
  and struggles between retail modes
    of production, 33
Standard Industrial Classification
    (SIC) Manual, 3–4
State policy, 140
Stop & Shop, 73, 110; *see also*
    Bradlees
Suburban markets, 20, 31, 70–71,
    115

Taxes, 140
Teamsters union, 110
Technology, new, 3, 36–37, 47, 98,
    112–15, 146–47, 151; *see also*
    EDP
  and economies of scale, 66
  and retail modes of production,
    6–7, 18, 23, 29
T.J. Maxx, 15
Training programs, 64, 111–112, 139,
    148
Transportation factor, 113, 115

Unions, 110–11
United Food and Commercial
    Workers of America, 8, 110
U.S. Social Security Administration,
    8
U.S. Supreme Court decisions, 128

Ventura Stores, Inc., 24
Vertical integration, 75
Virginia Dare stores, 13

Wages, 87, 98–106, 108–109,
    117–19, 135, 144–45, 148
  and decline of commission selling,
    109–10
  and unions, 110–11
Women, in retail labor force, 80,
    83–84, 88–92, 95–96, 149

wages, 99–101, 103–105
Woolworth, F.W., 48, 51, 119

Youth, in retail industry, 80, 83–84,
    90–91, 95–96, 149; *see also* Age,
    Labor force
  and wages, 99–101, 107

Zayre, 12, 15, 68, 70, 136